By the Editors of Consumer Guide®

Crown Publishers, Inc. • New York

Contents

Copyright© 1978 by Publications International, Ltd.
All rights reserved.
This book may not be reproduced or quoted in whole or in part by mimeograph or any other printed means or for presentation on radio or television without written permission from:
Louis Weber, President
Publications International, Ltd.
3841 West Oakton Street
Skokie, Illinois 60076
Permission is never granted for commercial purposes.

Manufactured in the United States of America
1 2 3 4 5 6 7 8 9 10

Published by Crown Publishers, Inc.
One Park Avenue, New York, N.Y. 10016

Library of Congress Cataloging in Publication Data
Main entry under title:

Smoke cookery.

  Includes index
    1. Cookery (Smoked foods)   2. Kitchen utensils.
I. Consumer Guide
TX835.S58   641.5'8   77-11717
ISBN 0-517-53153-4
ISBN 0-517-54154-2 pbk.

Cover Design: Frank E. Peiler
Photography: Bill Miller
Illustrations: Janice Saltz

Successful Smoke-Cooking

Smoke-cooking is not grilling, not broiling, not baking, not steaming and not really smoking.

It is cooking at very low temperatures (usually between 200°F and 250°F), with the addition of smoke from smoldering bits of aromatic woods. The smoke adds flavor but does not cook the food. Smoke-cooking starts, as does any cooking, with a heat source. Most smoke cookers use charcoal, many use an electric element, some are convertible. The heat source is at the bottom of the cylinder-shaped smoke cooker. The smoker is open at the bottom for air and covered at the top to hold in heat and smoke.

Just slightly above the fire pan which holds the burning charcoal or the glowing electric element, is a water pan. During cooking it is filled with water, a marinade or other flavorings. You can cook vegetables in the water pan as the main dish cooks on the grill. The grill that holds the main dish is located directly above the water pan. The water in the pan absorbs and tempers the intense heat from the charcoal or electricity, creating a low, moist and even heat that cooks the food on the cooking grill gently and slowly. The water does

reach simmering and does steam slightly, but not so much that the food cooks by steam. As the food cooks, the drippings fall into the water pan, creating flavorful juices. As the juices simmer they add additional flavor to the cooking food. The liquid left in the water pan at the end of the cooking time can be the base for a superb gravy or sauce.

The whole principle is somewhat like the *mirepoix* that chefs use when roasting meat. *Mirepoix* is a combination of finely chopped vegetables arranged in a roasting pan. The meat goes on top of the vegetables, or on a rack over them. The drippings then flavor the vegetables and the resulting combination of vegetables and juices is used to make savory sauces.

The smoke comes from chunks, chips or twigs of dried wood, soaked to prevent them from burning, then added to the fire pan. As the wood smolders, its aromatic smoke swirls up around the food on the cooking grill, adding flavor.

Smoke-cooking, you see, is not smoking. Smoking merely flavors and preserves at temperatures below those needed to cook foods. Thus "smoked" hams and bacon must be cooked before eating. In contrast, smoke-cooking actually cooks foods, with the added bonus of flavor from the smoke. The food preparation is simple, the fire-building is simple and the cooking itself effortless. And, unlike barbecue grilled or brazier-cooked foods, the cooking is long, slow and easy.

The change in timing takes the greatest adjustment when you begin to smoke-cook. Smoke-cooking requires an adjustment in timing from minutes or an hour or two, to several hours or all day — much like learning to use a slow-cooker.

The temperatures of smoke-cooking are about half that of normal oven roasting, so it is a safe rule of thumb to figure it will take twice as long to smoke-cook as to cook in a range oven. The recipes in this book give cooking times. Every smoke cooker we tested is accompanied by an instruction booklet which gives charts and times for cooking in that particular smoker.

The advantages to smoke-cooking are many. First, the flavor is delicious, so delicious that you probably will have smoke-cooked foods at least once a week. Smoke-cooked turkey is likely to become a holiday tradition. A second advantage is the ease of cooking. Once you have prepared the food and started the fire the rest is fuss-free. You may have to check the water pan and add water after about four hours of cooking, but otherwise you leave the cooker alone. A third advantage is that using a smoke cooker outside keeps your kitchen cool. As an extra bonus it frees your range oven for other jobs, a particularly important factor at busy holidays, for example.

The disadvantages to smoke-cooking are few. Finding a suitable place to smoke-cook and store the smoker may be a problem. With one exception, they are taller than many charcoal grills, and require patio or yard space. Because you can use a smoker outside all year, you may prefer to keep it readily at hand. Otherwise you will need to set aside a corner of the garage for storage. Many models can be broken down and repacked in their original boxes for storing, taking up about the same amount of space as a spare tire.

Smoke-Cooking Recipes

Smoke-cooking is easy! Most recipes in this book have two separate parts: the first part tells how to prepare the food, usually with a marinade or seasonings; the second part tells how to cook it. The second part of the recipes follows the same sequence with minor variations. Once the food is in the smoker, you can disappear. Depending on the recipe and the brand of cooker you have, you can take off for several hours and come back to a

tender, savory and very delicious smoked main course. If you are really clever, you will have all the other ingredients of a great meal waiting in the refrigerator, so that all you have to do is take the meat out of the smoker, carve and serve it.

Timing

The timing of smoke-cooking is, like the cooking itself, relaxed and easy. Allow plenty of time. Many variables affect the cooking time, so always allow too much time rather than too little. Smoke-cooked foods will stay moist, juicy and tender for an hour or so in the cooker. Be sure there is water in the water pan, because that is the secret to keeping the food moist. The type of charcoal you use, the temperature of the food, the outside temperature and wind, and the altitude all influence the cooking time, so you are at the mercy of all these elements.

Judge the weather and alter the cooking times accordingly. The times given in most manufacturer's directions, and in our recipes, are for ideal conditions: outside temperature 70°F or above and only gentle breezes. Cold or windy weather and high altitude mean cooking will take longer, particularly with charcoal units.

This means that you will be wise to plan some appetizers, and perhaps some activities, to fill that hour that you may have on your hands. Plenty of beverages are always an easy way to help cover up the delay, but have some food ready for pre-dinner nibbling, too. You want to be sure your guests are in a condition to savor the food, when it comes. Go Californian and have a jumbo salad to start with. Dips, assorted fresh crisp vegetables (the French call them *crudites*), cheeses, crackers, or any of the appetizers from the recipes in this book, make delicious starters for a smoke-cooked meal.

Making a Meal

Fixing a feast in your smoke cooker also means planning some complementary foods to round out the meal. Because smoke-cooked foods usually have such rich and savory flavors, mild-flavored accompaniments are in order. It is fun to smoke cook a vegetable along with the meat, or perhaps start out with a smoked appetizer, but one or two other smoked items are usually enough. On each page, along with the recipe for a smoke-cooked dish, you will find an additional recipe to complement the smoked food. Sometimes the additional recipe is for using leftover smoked meat. We hope the extra recipes help you to fully enjoy smoke-cooked foods.

Tools to Make Smoke-Cooking Easier

There are several tools and gadgets that can simplify and improve your smoke-cooking.

Meat Thermometer. There is no better way to judge how well done meat is than with a good quality meat thermometer which has been kept clean and in working order. Always remember to insert the thermometer into the center of the largest muscle of the meat, with the point away from bone and fat.

Protective Mitts. You will prevent many burns (or dropped pieces of food) by safeguarding your hands with big, thick mitts. Keep them close to the cooker, so they are always there when you need them.

Long-Handled Turner and Tongs. Moving hot food in and out of a smoker, or moving food around the smoker's grill, can be dangerous. Select tools with handles or hooks on the end, so you can hang them where you are working.

Heatproof Trays. When you move food from the cooker to the kitchen for carving, you will need something sturdy and heatproof to hold it.

Carving Set. Proper carving is just as important as proper cooking, so work with a good, sharp knife and a sturdy holding fork.

Other Equipment. Heavy-duty foil, heavy-duty plastic bags to hold food as it marinates, and a grill cleaner are all helpful.

Smoke, Fire and Safety

Any cooking outside requires special precautions. Place your smoke cooker out of the way of traffic and warn family and guests that the smoke cooker's dome is hot. If toddlers are around, it would be a good idea to fence in the smoke cooker or keep the toddlers indoors.

The smoke cooker should be put on a heatproof surface, preferably on a handy ash guard, drip guard, large piece of aluminum foil or layers of newspaper. If you have a patch of yard that will not be bothered by a little heat and some ashes, place the smoker there. Most charcoal smokers have a hole in the bottom where a few ashes will come out. Some units will drip condensed steam down the sides and drops could discolor a light-colored patio.

When you start a charcoal fire there will be some flames, so place the unit away from trees or bushes. Then, when you add the soaked wood to the hot coals there will be smoke, so keep your own and your neighbors' open windows in mind. Smoke-cooking on a balcony is not recommended because of the pervasive odor.

Smoke-cooking is a backyard or big patio activity, not for balconies or other close quarters. The smoke odor can linger for days.

Step-by-Step Directions for Charcoal Smokers

1. Always read the manufacturer's directions completely. Follow the instructions for assembling the smoke cooker. If any of the manufacturer's directions given for your smoke cooker differ from the instructions that follow, use the directions written specifically for the smoker you own.

2. Place the smoke cooker outside on a level surface, out of the way of children or traffic and somewhat away from the house. There will be flames if you use a charcoal lighter fluid to start the fire and there will be some smoke, particularly at the beginning of cooking. Set the smoker on a heatproof surface, ash guard, or piece of foil. Some steam condenses and drips down as the smoker cooks; the drops of liquid can stain a patio. Also, a smoker with holes in the fire pan will shed some ashes.

3. Follow the manufacturer's directions for any first-time preparation of the smoke cooker, such as wiping the inside with oil.

4. Read the recipe through and prepare or marinate the meat or other ingredients as the recipe di-

2. Placement is important. Set the smoker outside on a level, heatproof surface.

5. Line the fire pan with foil for easy cleanup.

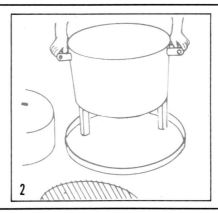

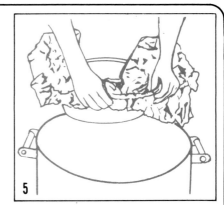

5. Be sure to make a hole in the foil, if there is a hole in the firepan.

6. Insert the fire pan in the bottom of the smoker.

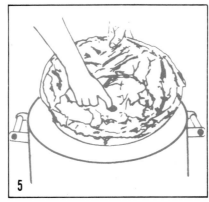

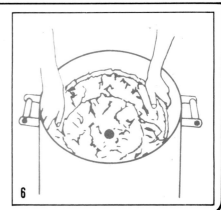

6. Fill the fire pan with good quality hardwood charcoal briquettes. The amount of charcoal depends on the length of smoke-cooking time.

7. Squirt about ½ to 1 cup odorless lighter fluid over the briquettes and let it soak in a few minutes.

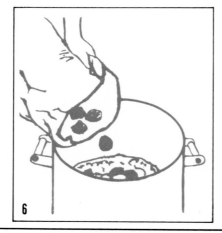

7. Light the charcoal.

8. Expect to wait about 30 minutes for the charcoal to be hot enough to smoke-cook. While waiting, spray the water pan and grill with pan coating or brush lightly with oil.

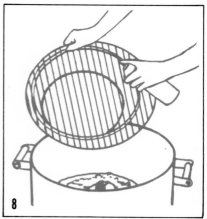

rects. Each recipe in this book gives you an approximate timetable of when to prepare the food and when to prepare the smoker.

5. Line the fire pan with foil to make cleaning easier, if you wish. If the fire pan has a hole in the bottom, be sure to poke a hole through the foil lining.

6. Insert the fire pan in the bottom of the smoker. Fill the fire pan with good-quality, hardwood charcoal briquettes. Most recipes require the fire pan to be filled level with its brim. If more or less charcoal is needed the recipe will tell you. The amount of charcoal is determined by the length of time it takes to cook the food.

7. Squirt or pour about ½ to 1 cup of odorless charcoal lighter fluid (not gasoline or any other flammable liquid) over the briquettes and let it soak in for a few minutes. Light the charcoal with a match. You could use an electric starter which eliminates the need for lighter fluid.

8. It usually takes around 30 minutes for the charcoal to become hot enough for smoke-cooking. While you wait for the charcoal, spray the water

pan and cooking grill with pan coating or brush them lightly with oil. The water pan can be lined with foil for easy cleaning.

9. Start soaking 2 or 3 chunks of wood or a handful of wood chips in enough water to cover them. The wood should soak at least 15 minutes.

10. When the charcoal is hot and covered with grey ash (about 30 minutes from the time you lit it), take the wood from the water and shake it well to drain. Place the wood on the glowing, ash-covered coals.

11. Wearing heavy gloves or barbecue mitts, set the water pan in place.

12. Carefully pour hot tap water into the pan until it is almost full. If a recipe calls for marinade to be added to the water pan, be sure to leave enough room for it.

13. Set the cooking grill in place above the water pan.

14. Arrange the food in a single layer on the cooking grill. Leave some space between each piece of food, if possible, and do not let any pieces stick out over the edge of the water pan. Food that ex-

9. Start soaking 2 or 3 chunks of wood or a handful of wood chips. Soak for at least 15 minutes.

10. Place the drained wood on the hot, ash-covered charcoal.

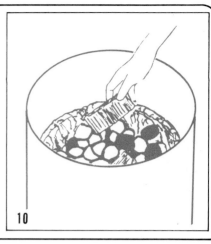

11. Wear heavy mitts to set the water pan in place.

12. Pour hot water carefully into the pan until it is almost full. Some recipes call for less water because marinade is added to the water pan.

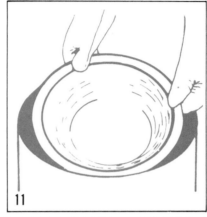

tends beyond the water pan will overcook. Insert a meat thermometer in large pieces of meat. The thermometer's tip should be in the center of the largest muscle, away from the bone or fat.

15. Close the cover on the smoker and cook according to the recipe you are following, or the instruction book that comes with your smoker.

16. Do not lift the cover until the end of the cooking time, unless the food has to cook for

13. Set the cooking grill in place above the water pan.

14. Food should be arranged in a single layer. Center single items on the grill.

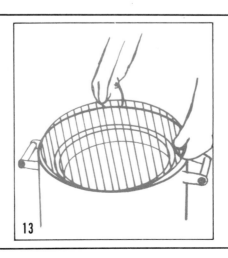

14. Insert a meat thermometer in large pieces of meat.

15. Cover the smoker. Remember, no peeking! Wait until the end of the cooking time to lift off the cover, unless you have to add water.

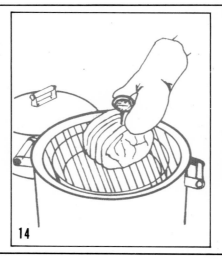

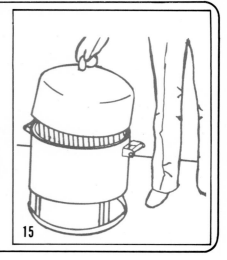

more than 4 hours and you need to add water to the water pan.

17. If the food does have to cook more than 4 hours, check the water pan to make sure it has not gone dry. There are three ways to check the water pan without lifting the lid. The easiest way is to check the heat indicator, if your smoker has one.

The heat indicator will register in the upper range of cooking or in the "Hot" section, if the water pan is empty. If your smoker does not have a heat indicator, put your ear fairly close to the smoker and listen for the sizzle and pop of juices as they hit the empty water pan. If you can hear sizzling, you need to add water to the pan. The third way

17. The smoker becomes extremely hot when the water evaporates. Hold your hand near but not touching the smoker to check if the water pan needs more water.

18. If so, quickly lift lid and add water.

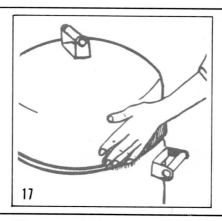

20. Always lift the lid away from you so steam will not scald your face.

20. Check food to see if it has reached the desired doneness.

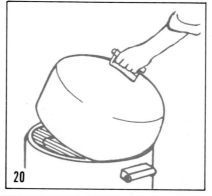

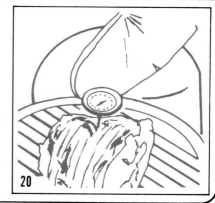

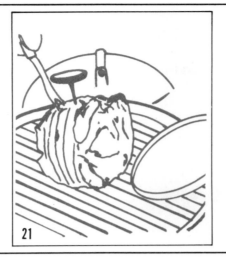

21. Wear heavy mitts when lifting food from the smoker.

25. Lift the fire pan out of the smoker and put the smoker's cover over it to smother the coals.

to tell if the water has evaporated is to place your hand near, but not touching, the smoker. When the water pan is dry, the sides of the smoker become very hot.

18. To refill the water pan, have a container full of hot tap water ready. Quickly lift the lid and carefully pour the water through the cooking grill and into the water pan. Cover the smoke cooker immediately and continue to cook. Add at least 15 minutes to the total cooking time for each time you lift the lid. Check the water pan every 4 hours.

19. Some foods require more than 7 hours of smoke-cooking, and you may need to replenish the coals. See the directions in "Crisis Cooking" for adding hot coals to the smoke cooker.

20. When the cooking time is up, carefully lift the cover, tilting it away from you so the steam will not scald your face. Check the food to see if it is done. Refer to the recipe for "doneness" tests. If the food is not done, continue cooking, or see "Crisis Cooking" for suggestions.

21. Wearing heavy gloves or barbecue mitts, or using long-handled tongs, lift the food from the cooking grill to a heated platter or cutting board when it is done. Second helpings can be kept warm in the covered smoker.

22. If you are going to use the juices in the water pan for gravy or sauce, carefully lift out the water pan and follow one of the recipes in the "Gravy" section.

23. If you are not keeping second helpings warm, lift out the cooking grill and set it aside to clean later. You can wrap the cooking grill in several layers of wet newspaper to "soak" while you eat.

24. After you have finished cooking, after the second helpings have been served and after any additional leftovers have been safely wrapped and refrigerated, you may wish to use the coals that are left to smoke-flavor foods. See the chapter on "Smoke-Flavor" for recipes.

25. If you are not going to smoke-flavor food, it is time to smother the fire. You can let the coals die out on their own, but by smothering them the fire will go out sooner and you may also save some charcoal to use another time. Wearing gloves or barbecue mitts, carefully lift the fire pan out of the smoke cooker and set it on a heatproof surface. Put the smoke cooker's cover over the fire pan and leave it alone for several hours, until the fire pan is cold to the touch.

26. Dump the ashes into a plastic garbage bag or onto your compost heap, picking out any unburned charcoal briquettes to store in a plastic bag for another cooking session. Be sure all ashes and coals are cold before throwing them out or storing them.

27. Wash the water pan and cooking grill in hot suds or in the dishwasher. Rinse and dry them. If you wish, wipe the outside of the smoke cooker with a sudsy cloth. It is not necessary to clean the inside of the smoker.

For Successful Smoke-Cooking in Charcoal Smokers

Always be sure to allow plenty of cooking time. Almost every food can wait an hour or so beyond the recommended time in the low, moist heat of the smoke cooker. However, if you underestimate the cooking time, your guests may not want to wait. The safe choice is to select the maximum cooking time, if a range is given. As long as the water pan is more than half way full, cooked food will stay hot, moist and tender.

You probably will need to increase the cooking time by 1/2 to 1 1/2 hours under the following circumstances.

- The temperature is below 65°F.
- It is very windy.
- You live 3500 feet or more above sea level.
- You have used poor quality or poorly stored charcoal.
- The charcoal is damp.

Charcoal

High quality hardwood charcoal briquettes are one of the keys to successful smoke-cooking. Poor quality charcoal does not burn as well, as hot or as long. Off brand specials may have an attractive price, but it is best to stick to a brand that you know will work. Charcoal fresh from the store is best because, hopefully, it has been handled and stored properly. For home storage, be sure to keep the charcoal dry. A partial bag of briquettes that has been left out in the rain will not burn well, if at all, even though it has had a chance to dry out. Store any leftover charcoal in the bag, tightly closed, in a dry place. A corner of the garage is fine, or an outside shed, if the bag is up off the ground.

Lighting Charcoal

You can use an electric charcoal starter to get your fire going. Just follow the manufacturer's directions. Or, use special charcoal lighter fluid or jelly. Do not use gasoline, kerosene or other flammable liquids! They are dangerous. In addition they have distinctive odors that will flavor the food.

Squirt the fluid evenly over coals, using about 1 cup for 10 pounds of briquettes. Let the fluid soak into the coal for a few minutes before lighting it with a match.

Give the coals about 30 minutes to get going before starting to cook. The briquettes will be covered with grey ash and you will be able to feel the heat coming off them.

Wood

The smoke from special woods is what gives smoke-cooked foods their unique flavor and color. A few manufacturers of electric smoke cookers

Twigs, chunks, or wood chips may be used.

direct you not to soak wood before adding, but most electric smokers and all charcoal models take wood that has been soaked for 15 to 30 minutes. This pre-soaking keeps the wood from burning quickly and instead lets it smolder slowly.

You can buy wood for smoke-cooking at the supermarket, at outdoor shops or wherever smoke cookers are sold. Many of the smoke cooker manufacturers offer mail-order bags of wood. This wood comes in chips — (large coin sized pieces, usually of hickory); or fist-sized chunks, also usually hickory. Our recipes call for wood to be added by the handful of chips or number of chunks.

You can use wood from your own trees, if you wish. Cut the wood into chips or chunks, or use finger-sized sticks, about three or four inches long in place of each handful or chunk called for in the recipe. If you use fully dried wood, soak it for about 15 to 30 minutes. You can use green sticks or twigs, directly from the tree, without any pre-soaking.

Use only woods from deciduous trees (those that shed their leaves). Wood from pine, cedar or other evergreen trees contains pitch and resin, both of which will discolor and make foods taste bad. Do not use them.

Use hickory, mesquite, apple, cherry, peach or other fruit woods; wood from other nut bearing trees, such as oak, walnut; or try aspen or alder. Southerners like to use palmetto, mangrove or mesquite, while Midwesterners often dry corn cobs to use. The choice is yours. Experiment, if you wish, to see which you prefer. Or you can stick with the bag of chips from the store.

You can dry wood to use for smoking in a charcoal smoke cooker. Follow the directions for smoke flavoring: remove water pan, put cooking grill back in place and put the twigs or sticks (or corncobs) on the cooking grill above very low coals left after cooking. Leave the wood on the grill until it is very dry. Soak as directed above before using the wood for smoke-cooking.

Crisis Cooking

When smoke-cooking foods in a charcoal cooker there are many, many factors that can affect the cooking time: the charcoal itself, how it has been stored, how it is lit, and how it is arranged in the fire pan. The efficiency of both charcoal and electric smokers is affected by the outside temperature, the wind, rain, the temperature of the food and the mass of the food. Because there are so many variables, it is possible for cooking times to be much longer than the range of times given in the recipes.

Here are some steps to meet those rare occasions when food takes much longer to cook than you expect.

The most expedient step is to take the food out of the smoker and move it to your range oven (or microwave, if you have it) to finish cooking. If you are waiting for a large piece of meat, cut it into

2. Place 4 to 5 pounds of charcoal in the center of an old pan, or in a pan made from heavy-duty foil.

3. Squirt charcoal with lighter fluid.

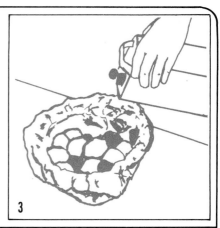

3. Light the fluid-soaked charcoal.

6. Carefully remove the food, grill and water pan. When the coals are ready, dump them into the fire pan.

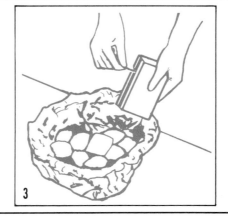

smaller pieces and roast or broil it in your oven to finish.

You can also add additional hot coals to the fire pan in order to finish the cooking in the smoker.

1. Find a container, such as an old metal pan, a large can or other heatproof and expendable container, or make a pan from several layers of heavy-duty foil.

2. Pile about 4 to 5 pounds of charcoal in the center of the pan.

3. Squirt the charcoal with charcoal lighter fluid and light the fluid-soaked coals, or ignite with an electric starter.

4. Wearing oven mitts, carefully lift out the food and cooking grill and set them aside.

5. Carefully lift out the water pan and set it aside.

6. After about 20 minutes, when coals are very hot and covered with grey ash, carefully dump the hot coals into the fire pan, or add them to the fire pan with long-handled tongs.

7. Replace the water pan, cooking grill, food. Cover the smoker. Continue to cook until done.

Step-by-Step Directions for Electric Smokers

1. Always read the manufacturer's directions completely. Follow the instructions for assembling the smoke cooker. If any of the manufacturer's directions given for your smoke cooker differ from the instructions that follow, use the directions written for your electric smoker.

2. Place the smoker outside on a level surface, out of the way of children or traffic and close to an electric outlet. (Check the manufacturer's directions; some require a 110V AC outlet, others need a 120V AC outlet.) Set the smoker on a heatproof surface, over a drip pan, piece of foil or layers of newpaper to catch the slight amount of dripping from condensed steam. The drops of liquid can stain an unprotected patio. If you must use an extension cord, be sure it is a heavy-duty outdoor cord. Arrange the cord so it cannot trip anyone.

Some manufacturers suggest that electric smoke cookers can be used indoors. Testing showed that the aroma of smoke, while subtle, is strong enough to make cooking indoors unpleasant. Cooking in the smoker without adding wood can be done indoors, near a fireplace or a vent fan; cooking in a well ventilated garage is also possible if you do not add wood.

3. Follow the manufacturer's directions for any first-time preparation of the smoke cooker, such as wiping the inside with oil, spraying the inside with pan coating or preheating the smoker.

4. Read the recipe through and prepare or marinate the meat or ingredients as the recipe directs. Each recipe in this book gives you an approximate timetable of when to prepare the food and when to prepare the smoker. Obviously, with an electric smoker you do not need to wait for the coals to get hot; you can put the food on the grill as soon as the food is ready.

All foods must be completely thawed or the cooking times will be much longer. You can take meat from the refrigerator to stand at room temperature while you assemble any other ingredients or prepare the water pan.

5. Follow the manufacturer's directions for soaking the wood. Some electric cookers call for dry wood. If the wood is to be soaked, put it in enough water to cover for 15 to 30 minutes. Use a handful of wood chips or 2 or 3 chunks of wood unless the recipe directs otherwise. Lift the wood from the water and shake well to drain before putting it in the smoker. Place the wood chips or chunks on their special pan, positioned as the manufacturer directs.

6. Spray the water pan and cooking grill with pan coating or brush them lightly with oil.

7. Put the water pan in place and carefully pour in

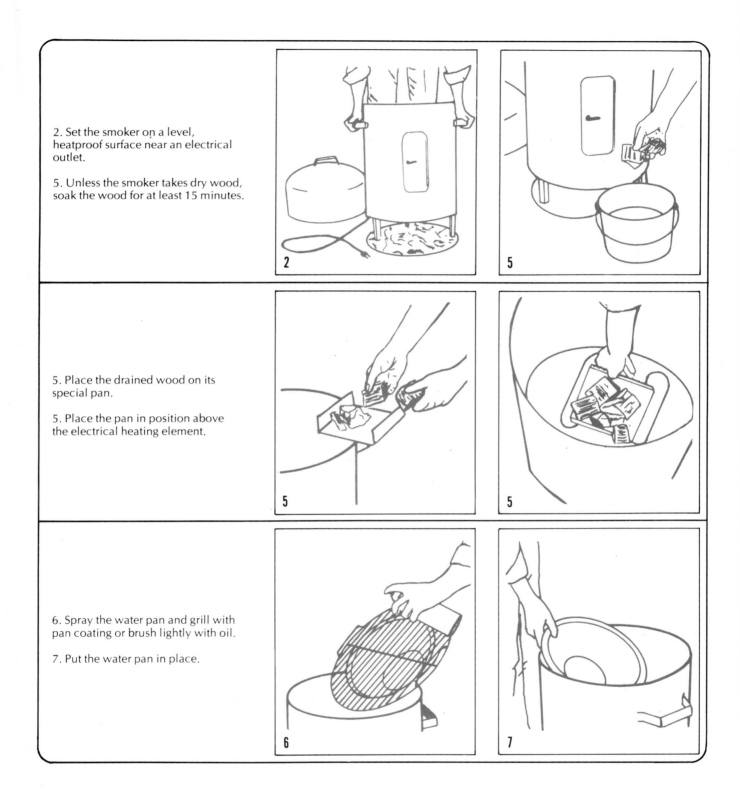

2. Set the smoker on a level, heatproof surface near an electrical outlet.

5. Unless the smoker takes dry wood, soak the wood for at least 15 minutes.

5. Place the drained wood on its special pan.

5. Place the pan in position above the electrical heating element.

6. Spray the water pan and grill with pan coating or brush lightly with oil.

7. Put the water pan in place.

hot tap water until it is almost full. If the recipe calls for marinade to be added to the water pan, be sure to leave enough room for it.

8. Set the cooking grill in place above the water pan.

9. Arrange the food in a single layer on the cooking grill. Leave some space between each piece of food, if possible. Do not let any pieces stick out over the edge of the water pan, or those parts will overcook. Insert a meat thermometer in large pieces of meat. The tip should be in the center of the largest muscle, away from bone or fat.

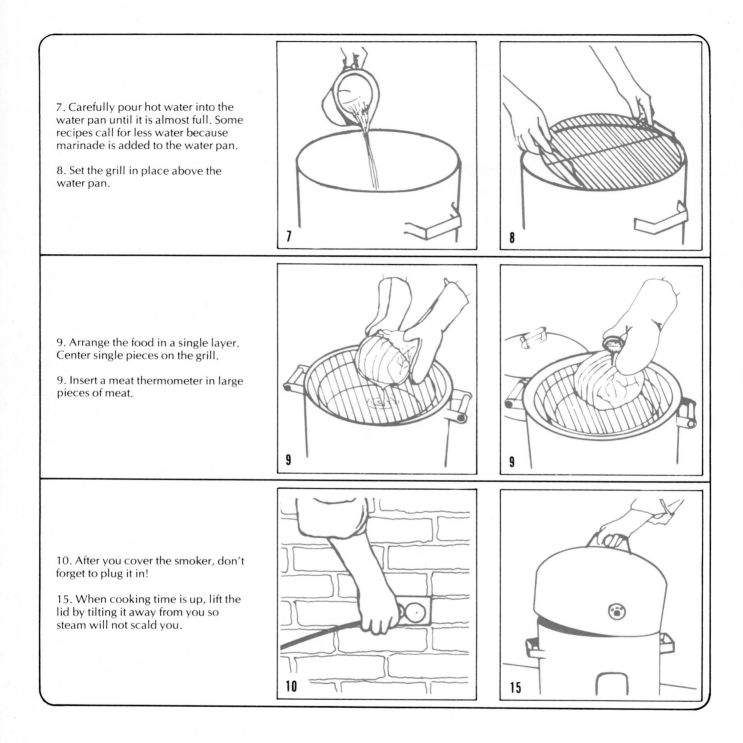

7. Carefully pour hot water into the water pan until it is almost full. Some recipes call for less water because marinade is added to the water pan.

8. Set the grill in place above the water pan.

9. Arrange the food in a single layer. Center single pieces on the grill.

9. Insert a meat thermometer in large pieces of meat.

10. After you cover the smoker, don't forget to plug it in!

15. When cooking time is up, lift the lid by tilting it away from you so steam will not scald you.

10. Place the cover over the smoke cooker and plug it in. Use the smoker on a circuit by itself. Should you plug in another appliance on the same circuit, you might blow a fuse or trip a circuit.

11. Cook the food according to the time chart in this book, the instruction book that comes with your smoker, or according to the recipe.

12. Do not lift the cover until the end of the cooking time, unless the food has to cook for more than 4 hours and the water pan drys out.

13. If the food does have to cook more than 4 hours, check the water pan to make sure it has not gone dry. There are three ways to check the water pan without lifting the lid. The easiest way is to check the heat indicator, if your smoker has one. The heat indicator will register in the upper range of cooking or in the "Hot" section, if the water pan is empty. If your smoker does not have a heat

indicator, put your ear fairly close to the smoker and listen for the sizzle and pop of juices as they hit the empty water pan. If you can hear sizzling, you need to add water to the pan. The third way to tell if the water has evaporated is to place your hand near (but not touching) the smoker. When the water pan is dry, the sides of the smoker become very hot.

14. To refill the water pan, have a container full of hot tap water ready. Quickly lift the lid and carefully pour the water through the cooking grill and into the water pan. Cover the smoke cooker immediately and continue to cook. Add at least 15 minutes to the total cooking time for each time you lift the lid. Check the water pan every 4 hours.

15. When the cooking time is up, carefully lift the cover, tilting it away from you so the steam will not scald your face. Check the food to see if it is done. (Refer to the recipe or manufacturer's instructions for "doneness" tests.) Cooking times are much less variable with electric smokers than with charcoal ones, but there is some variation between brands of electric smokers. Also, if the outside temperature is below 65°F, if you live 3500 feet or more above sea level, or if there is a variation in electric power on your line, you may need to cook food an extra hour or so.

Clean-Up

As soon as you have finished cooking, remove the cooking grill and water pan. Use the juices in the water pan for gravy, or discard them. Should there

be a thick layer of fat on the liquid in the water pan, skim it off to dispose of as you would bacon drippings. Then just wash the pan as you would a saucepan, in hot suds or in the dishwasher.

You can soak the cooking grill in suds in a laundry tub, if you have one. Another trick is to soak several layers of newspaper with water and then sprinkle them with a little detergent. Wrap the cooking grill in the wet paper and set it aside to soak.

We like to use a product called a "grill cleaner," an abrasive pad attached to a plastic handle, that makes grill cleaning almost effortless.

The outside of your smoker needs just a wipe-off with a sudsy cloth, followed by a rinse with a damp cloth. Do this when the cooker has cooled off somewhat. Some cookers have lids designed so that condensation of steam and cooking juices from the lid run down the outside of the cooker. This will leave dark marks on the outside of the cooker. The stains are no problem with a brown or black cooker, but somewhat unsightly on a yellow or red one.

Because of the smoke, the inside of the unit is going to get sooty and dirty, and it can stay that way.

Always check manufacturer's directions for any special cleaning instructions, particularly on the electric heating elements. In the absence of any instructions for the electric element, simply wipe out the reflector pan (with the element unplugged, of course).

When you are not using your smoke cooker, assemble it with pans, grills and cover in place, then cover it all with a heavy-duty plastic garbage bag. Set it aside in an out-of-the-way place.

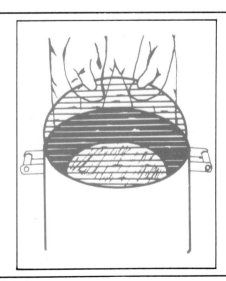 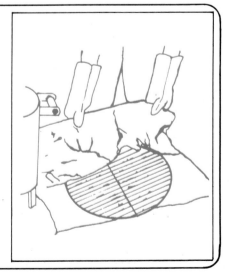

Wear oven mitts to remove the grill and water pan when cooking is over. Wash the pan as you would a saucepan. Cleaning the grill is easier if it soaks first in layers of wet newspaper that have been sprinkled with detergent.

Smoke-Cooking Time Chart

Food and weight	Hours to Smoke-Cook	Doneness Test
Beef and Venison		
Boneless roasts:		
3-4 lbs.	3-4	use meat thermometer:
5-7 lbs.	5-7	140°F rare
8-10 lbs.	7-9	160°F medium
		170°F well done
Lamb		
Leg or shoulder		
roasts, 5-7 lbs.	5-7	use meat thermometer:
		175°F medium
		180°F well done
Pork		
Chops, 6-8 (1 in. thick)	3-4	meat pulls away from bone
Roast, 3-5 lbs.	5-7	use meat thermometer: 170°F
Roast, 5-7 lbs.	7-8	use meat thermometer: 170°F
Ribs, 5 lbs.	4-6	meat pulls away from bone
Ham		
Cooked, all sizes	3-5	use meat thermometer: 130°F
Fresh, 10 lbs.	7-10	use meat thermometer: 170°F
Chicken		
1 to 3 fryers, 2-2½ lbs. each:	4-5	leg moves easily in joint
whole, split or cut up		
1 or 2 roasters, 5 lbs. each:	6-8	leg moves easily in joint
Turkey and Goose		
Unstuffed, 8-12 lbs.	7-9	180°F or leg moves easily in joint
13-20 lbs.	10-12	leg moves easily in joint
Duck		
Unstuffed, 3-5 lbs.	5-6	leg moves easily in joint
Small Game Birds		
(as many as grill holds)	3-5	leg moves easily in joint
Fish		
Whole large, 6 lbs.	3-5	flakes with fork
Whole pan fish (as many as grill holds)	2-3	flakes with fork
Fillets (as many as grill holds)	2-3	flakes with fork
Steaks (as many as grill holds)	2-3	flakes with fork
Shrimp		
(as many as grill holds)	1-2	firm, white flesh
Lobster Tails		
(as many as grill holds)	1-3	firm, white flesh

BEEF

Bring on the important guests, the discriminating gourmets, the picky eaters and the hungry hordes! Smoked beef appeals to everyone's palate. Smoke-cooking enhances all cuts of beef, from pot roasts to short ribs. Marinades add special accents, such as the tang of barbecue sauce and the flavor of blue cheese. Appetizer Steak Strips and Deviled Beef are just a few of the unusual recipes.

Roman Roast

A rich and herby marinade makes any boneless beef roast something very special. You can cook beef to your taste in the smoke-cooker. Use a meat thermometer to let you know when it reaches the stage you prefer. When the thermometer reaches 140°F meat is rare, at 160°F it is medium and at 170°F it is well done.

2/3 **cup red wine**
1/2 **cup chopped onion**
1/2 **cup chopped green**
    pepper
1/4 **cup oil**
2 **teaspoons basil**
2 **teaspoons salt**
1 **clove garlic, minced**
1 **(4½ to 5½-pound) boneless beef roast, rolled and tied**

The Night Before Serving

1. Combine all the ingredients except the roast in a deep bowl or large, heavy-duty plastic bag.
2. Place the meat in the bowl and turn it so all surfaces are covered with the marinade.
3. Cover with plastic wrap or close bag securely.
4. Refrigerate overnight, turning the meat in the marinade occasionally, if you think of it.

About 5 to 6 Hours Before Serving

1. Remove the meat from the refrigerator. Insert the meat thermometer with the tip in the center of the largest muscle, away from bone and fat.
2. Start soaking 2 or 3 chunks of wood or a handful of wood chips, unless the smoker takes dry wood.
3. Fill the fire pan full of charcoal briquettes and start the fire.
4. When the coals turn grey, drain the wood pieces and add them to the coals. (For electric units: unless the smoker takes dry wood, drain the wood pieces and put them in their special pan.)
5. Put the water pan in place and fill it about 3/4 full with hot water.
6. Set the cooking grill in place.
7. Place the meat in the center of the cooking grill and add the marinade to the water pan.
8. Cover. (Plug in electric smoker.) Smoke-cook about 4 to 5 hours or until the roast is done to your taste.
9. Cut the roast in thin slices to serve.

Makes 8 to 10 servings

It only takes a few ingredients to make a savory marinade for Roman Roast—onion, green pepper, basil and garlic are mixed with red wine and oil.

Mixing the marinade can be simplified by using a heavy-duty plastic bag. Pour all the ingredients into the bag.

Place the meat in the bag with the marinade, turning to coat all sides. Close the bag securely and refrigerate it overnight, turning the meat occasionally, if you think of it.

The juicy roast is ready for an imperial dinner, Roman-style.

Pot Roast with the Works

Pot roast does not cook to fork-tenderness in a smoke cooker as it does when braised in liquid; but, if you slice it thinly across the grain, you never know the difference. This unique topping is popular with all ages.

1 (3- or 4-pound) pot roast
1 cup chili sauce or 1 can (8 ounces) tomato sauce with onions
¼ cup sweet or dill pickle relish
2 tablespoons prepared mustard
1 teaspoon salt
⅛ teaspoon hot pepper sauce

About 4½ to 5 Hours Before Cooking

1. Remove the meat from the refrigerator and let it stand while preparing the fire.
2. Start soaking 2 or 3 chunks of wood or a handful of wood chips, unless the smoker takes dry wood.
3. Fill the fire pan full with charcoal briquettes and start the fire.
4. Combine the chili sauce, relish, mustard, salt and hot pepper sauce. Spread the mixture over the top of the pot roast.
5. When the coals turn grey, drain the wood pieces and add them to the coals. (For electric units: unless the smoker takes dry wood, drain the wood pieces and put them in their special pan.)
6. Put the water pan in place and fill almost full with hot water.
7. Put the cooking grill in place.
8. Put the pot roast in the center of the cooking grill.
9. Cover. (Plug in electric smoker.) Smoke-cook about 4 to 5 hours. After about 4 hours, you may need to check the water pan and add a quart or so of hot water.

Makes about 4 servings

Mix together the classic all-American condiments — chili sauce, pickle relish and mustard — to make a thick sauce.

Pour the savory sauce over the top of the pot roast and spread it to the edge of the meat.

When your smoke cooker is ready, place the roast in the center of the grill and smoke-cook 4 to 5 hours.

Pot Roast with the Works goes well with picnic fare. Slice the roast across the grain for tender eating.

Appetizer Steak Strips

Since large cuts of meat may take longer than expected to smoke-cook, it is a good idea to have some appetizers on hand to appease hungry guests. You can broil these marinated strips, or smoke-cook them over the water pan. The choice depends on how soon you would like to eat them.

1 pound skirt steak or flank steak cut crosswise into ½-inch wide strips
¼ cup red wine
¼ cup soy sauce
2 tablespoons oil

About 4 to 5 Hours Before Serving

1. Arrange the steak strips in a baking dish or heavy-duty plastic bag.
2. Combine all the remaining ingredients and pour them over the steak strips. Turn the strips once to coat all sides.
3. Cover the dish with plastic wrap or close the bag securely and marinate about an hour.
4. Lift the strips from the marinade and weave on skewers.
5. Add the strips to the cooking grill along with the main dish during the last 2 or 3 hours of cooking time, or broil them over hot coals, turning once, about 3 to 4 minutes on each side.

Makes about 6 appetizer servings

Appetizer Steak Strips make a handsome presentation with smoke-flavored cheese, nuts and seeds.

Red wine, soy sauce and a little oil make a tasty marinade. Mix them together and pour the marinade over the steak strips in a baking dish or heavy-duty plastic bag.

After about an hour of marinating, weave the steak strips on skewers.

Here the extra marinade is poured over the skewered meat into the water pan where it will add extra flavor to the smoke-cooking.

BEEF

Bordeaux Beef Roast

The easy marinade adds delightful flavor. You can let the meat marinate for a few hours or overnight. The marinade will add more flavor if you poke the meat in several places with a two-tined fork. The rich-tasting smoked beef needs a crunchy, tart accompaniment such as the accompanying chutney recipe. Dijon-style mustard would be a good choice to serve, too. Silver Turban Apples from the "Smoker Side Dish" chapter would be an easy smoke-along dessert for Bordeaux Beef Roast.

1 (5-pound) boneless beef rump roast
½ cup red wine
1 envelope onion soup mix

The Night Before Serving
1. Put the roast in a large, heavy-duty plastic bag.
2. Pour in the wine and onion soup mix.
3. Close the bag securely and then move it from hand to hand to mix the marinade and coat the meat on all sides.
4. Refrigerate overnight.

About 6 Hours Before Serving
1. Remove the meat from the refrigerator.
2. Start soaking 2 or 3 chunks of wood or a handful of wood chips, unless the smoker takes dry wood.
3. Fill the fire pan full with charcoal briquettes and start the fire.
4. When the coals turn grey, drain the wood pieces and add them to the coals. (For electric units: unless the smoker takes dry wood, drain the wood pieces and put them in their special pan.)
5. Put the water pan in place and fill about ¾ full with hot water.
6. Put the cooking grill in place.
7. Put the meat in the center of the cooking grill. Add the marinade to the water pan.
8. Cover. (Plug in electric smoker.) Smoke-cook about 5½ hours or until as done as you like. Use a meat thermometer to check doneness, if you wish. Insert the thermometer with the tip in the center of the largest muscle, away from fat. After about 4 hours, you may need to check the water pan and add a quart or so of hot water.

Makes about 10 servings

Fresh Chutney to go with Bordeaux Beef Roast

A sweet-sour chutney is an excellent relish to accompany Bordeaux Beef Roast or other smoked meats. This chutney also could be mixed with mayonnaise for a spunky salad dressing, used as a basting sauce for chicken, stirred into hot rice pilaf, or served with curries. If you have any leftover Bordeaux Beef Roast, you could serve it cold, buffet-style with assorted cheeses and — of course — Fresh Chutney. This chutney is not processed in a water bath and must be refrigerated.

Fresh Chutney to go with Bordeaux Beef Roast (continued)

½ **cucumber**
2 **green onions**
1 **apple, peeled and cored**
2 **cups cherry tomatoes, quartered**
1 **cup raisins**
1 **cup seedless grapes**
1 **teaspoon ground coriander**
1 **teaspoon salt**
¼ **teaspoon pepper**
1 **teaspoon grated orange rind**
1 **jar (10 ounces) red currant jelly**
1 **teaspoon prepared horseradish**

1. Chop the cucumber, onions and apple medium-fine.
2. Combine them with the tomatoes, raisins, grapes and seasonings in a large bowl.
3. Stir the grated orange peel into the fruit mixture.
4. Spoon the chutney into jars or other containers.
5. Heat the jelly and horseradish just until soft and stir until blended.
6. Spoon the jelly on top of the chutney in the containers. Cover and chill.

Makes about 7 cups

Bordeaux Beef Roast makes a marvelous meal.

BEEF

First Class Beef Roast

Whether or not marinades actually tenderize meat is a matter of debate; but there is no doubt that standing overnight in an assortment of spices and sauces does add extra-special flavor. You can use this marinade for other beef cuts, pork ribs or just as a brush-on sauce for burgers. A sharp carving knife is important to thin-slice the roast. To complete your "first class" menu, turn to the "Smoker Side Dishes" chapter for Asparagus in Foil and Smoker Mushrooms to go along with a crunchy green salad and perhaps a rice dish.

1 (5½-pound) boneless rolled and tied beef chuck or rump roast
1 can (8 ounces) tomato sauce
½ cup bottled steak sauce
3 tablespoons brown sugar
3 tablespoons red wine vinegar
1 tablespoon Worcestershire sauce

The Night Before Serving

1. Put the roast in a deep glass bowl or a large, heavy-duty plastic bag.
2. In a small mixing bowl or measuring cup, combine the remaining ingredients and mix until the sugar dissolves.
3. Pour the marinade over the roast. Turn the roast and spoon the marinade over it so all surfaces are covered.
4. Cover with plastic wrap or close the bag securely.
5. Refrigerate overnight, turning the meat in the marinade occasionally if you think of it.

About 6 Hours Before Serving

1. Remove the meat from the refrigerator.
2. Start soaking 2 or 3 chunks of wood or a handful of wood chips, unless the smoker takes dry wood.
3. Fill the fire pan with charcoal briquettes and start the fire.
4. When the coals turn grey, drain the wood pieces and add them to the coals. (For electric units: unless the smoker takes dry wood, drain the wood pieces and put them in their special pan.)
5. Put the water pan in place and fill it with hot water.
6. Put the cooking grill in place.
7. Lift the meat from the marinade and put it in the center of the cooking grill. Reserve the marinade to simmer and serve as a sauce, if desired.
8. Insert a meat thermometer with the point in the center of the thickest muscle.
9. Cover. (Plug in electric smoker.) Smoke-cook about 5 to 6 hours or until the meat thermometer reaches 140°F for rare, 160°F for medium or 170°F for well done. After about 4 hours, you may need to check the water pan and add a quart or so of hot water.

Makes about 10 servings

Supper in a Squash using First Class Beef Roast

Smoked beef is such a treat that even the leftovers are "first class." This recipe makes a quick supper by stuffing acorn squash with leftover smoked beef. For a delicious meal, put together a fruit or vegetable salad while the squash bakes.

Supper in a Squash using First Class Beef Roast (continued)

¼ **cup chopped onion**
¼ **cup chopped celery**
2 **tablespoons butter**
2 **to 3 cups diced leftover smoked beef**
1 **teaspoon salt**
⅛ **teaspoon pepper**
1 **cup soft whole wheat or rye bread crumbs**
2 **medium-sized acorn squash**
¼ **cup brown sugar**

1. Preheat the oven to 375°F.
2. Sauté the onion and celery in the butter just until the onion is limp.
3. Stir in the diced meat, salt, pepper and bread crumbs.
4. Cut the squash in half and make several shallow cuts in the surface flesh of each half.
5. Sprinkle the brown sugar in the squash halves and arrange them in a baking pan or dish.
6. Pile the meat mixture into the squash halves.
7. Cover with foil and bake 45 minutes.
8. Remove the foil and bake another 10 to 15 minutes or until the squash is tender.

Makes 4 servings

Blue Beef

Do you like the combination of beef and blue cheese? This easy marinade makes the most of both flavors and takes only minutes to prepare. If you are lucky enough to have any leftovers, you could cube the meat and skewer it on hors d'oeuvre picks alternated with cherry tomatoes, cocktail onions and baby gherkins for an instantly elegant appetizer course.

1 **(4-pound) boneless beef roast**
½ **cup oil**
½ **cup red wine vinegar**
1 **package (0.7 ounces) blue cheese salad dressing mix**
1 **tablespoon lemon juice**
1 **tablespoon Worcestershire sauce**
¼ **cup finely chopped parsley (optional)**

The Night Before Serving
1. Put the meat in a baking dish or heavy-duty plastic bag.
2. In a small mixing bowl or in a 1-pint measuring cup, combine all the remaining ingredients.
3. Pour the marinade over the meat. Turn the meat so it is completely coated with marinade.
4. Cover with plastic wrap or close the bag securely.
5. Refrigerate overnight.

About 5½ to 6 Hours Before Serving
1. Remove the meat from the refrigerator.
2. Start soaking 2 or 3 chunks of wood or a handful of wood chips, unless the smoker takes dry wood.
3. Fill the fire pan full with charcoal briquettes and start the fire. (For electric units: unless the smoker takes dry wood, drain the wood pieces and put them in their special pan.)
4. When the coals turn grey, drain the wood pieces and add them to the coals.
5. Put the water pan in place and fill it almost full with water.
6. Put the cooking grill in place.
7. Lift the meat from the marinade and put it in the center of the cooking grill. Pour the marinade into the water pan.
8. Cover. (Plug in electric smoker.) Smoke-cook about 5 hours or until the meat is firm to the touch. After about 4 hours, you may need to check the water pan and add a quart or so of hot water.
9. Cut the meat into thin slices to serve.

Makes 6 to 8 servings

BEEF

Snappy Potato Salad to go with Blue Beef

Spices and vinegar soak into the sliced potatoes, giving this salad a tantalizing flavor that contrasts well with Blue Beef. Smoker Roasted Corn on the Cob or Asparagus in Foil (see "Smoker Side Dishes"), and a fresh fruit dessert could round out your menu. Notice that the recipe calls for the potatoes to be peeled and sliced before cooking them, so they can absorb the seasoning while still hot.

5 **medium potatoes, peeled**	1. Slice the potatoes.
½ **cup vinegar**	2. Cook the potatoes in only enough water to cover for about 15 minutes or until just tender. Drain well.
1¼ **tablespoons mustard seed**	
1¼ **tablespoons celery seed**	3. Add the vinegar, mustard and celery seeds to the hot potatoes. Toss them gently to mix; cover and let them cool.
2 **large stalks celery**	
5 **green onions**	4. Chop the celery, onion and green pepper and add them to the potatoes.
1 **medium green pepper, seeded**	
4 **hard-cooked eggs**	5. Coarsely chop the eggs and add them to the potatoes along with the sour cream, salt and pepper.
1 **cup dairy sour cream or plain yogurt**	6. Toss the salad gently but thoroughly to mix.
1 to 2 **teaspoons seasoned salt**	7. Cover and chill thoroughly.
¼ **teaspoon pepper**	*Makes 6 to 8 servings*

Barbecued Flank Steak

Flank steak marinated in a snappy barbecue sauce and then smoke-cooked makes a mouth-watering main dish. The trick to serving tender flank steak isn't as much in the cooking as in the carving. Use a sharp carving knife and cut very thin slices, slanting and across the grain, almost as if you were whittling a stick to a point.

1 **flank steak (about 1½ pounds)**
⅓ **cup chili sauce**
¼ **cup vinegar or red wine**
1 **bay leaf, crushed**
1 **teaspoon onion salt**
½ **teaspoon pepper**

The Night Before Serving
1. Put the steak in a rectangular glass baking dish or heavy-duty plastic bag.
2. Combine all the remaining ingredients in a small bowl.
3. Pour the marinade over the steak and turn the steak several times to coat completely.

About 3 Hours Before Serving
1. Start soaking 2 or 3 chips, unless the smoker takes dry wood.
2. Remove the meat from the refrigerator and let it stand while preparing the fire.
3. Fill the fire pan full of charcoal briquettes and start the fire.
4. When coals turn grey, drain the wood pieces and add them to the coals. (For electric units: unless the smoker takes dry wood, drain the wood pieces and put them in their special pan.)
5. Put water pan in place and fill almost full with hot water.
6. Put the cooking grill in place.
7. Put steak in the center of the cooking grill.
8. Cover. (Plug in electric smoker.) Smoke-cook about 2½ to 3 hours.

Makes about 4 servings

Hot Spinach Salad to go with Barbecued Flank Steak

It is the piquant, bacon-flavored dressing that makes this salad an extraordinary partner for Barbecued Flank Steak. Water Pan Potatoes (see "Smoker Side Dishes"), butter-crusted rolls and fresh fruit for dessert could complete the menu for a pleasant family meal.

¾ **pound fresh spinach**
4 **slices bacon, chopped**
1½ **tablespoons flour**
1 **tablespoon sugar**
1¼ **teaspoons salt**
1 **cup chicken bouillon or water**
½ **cup cider vinegar**

1. Wash the spinach well. Drain; remove the tough stems.
2. Chop the spinach coarsely and set it aside in a large salad bowl.
3. In a skillet, cook the bacon until crisp.
4. Drain off all but 2 tablespoons of drippings. Leave the bacon pieces in the skillet.
5. Blend the flour, sugar and salt into the bacon and drippings in the skillet. Cook until frothy.
6. Stir in the bouillon and vinegar and cook and stir until smooth and thickened.
7. Pour the dressing over the spinach in the salad bowl and toss to mix. Serve immediately.

Makes 6 to 10 servings

Deviled Beef Ribs

Deviled Beef Ribs are for casual dining since they almost have to be held in your hand to be eaten. The kids probably will pretend they are eating bones from a prehistoric monster. Have lots of napkins available! These ribs are not short ribs, but back ribs which are cut from a standing rib roast when it is boned. Start with raw meat, as the recipe describes, or use the sauce for the leftover cooked ribs from a rib roast.

4 **pounds beef back ribs**
1 **can (15 ounces) tomato sauce with onions and green peppers**
¼ **cup vinegar**
2 **tablespoons prepared mustard**
1 **tablespoon prepared horseradish**
1 **teaspoon salt**
½ **teaspoon garlic powder**

The Night Before Serving
1. Put the ribs in a shallow baking dish or pan.
2. Combine all the remaining ingredients in a medium bowl and pour them over the ribs.
3. Turn the ribs to coat completely with marinade.
4. Cover with plastic wrap and refrigerate overnight.

About 6 Hours Before Serving
1. Remove the ribs from the refrigerator.
2. Start soaking 2 or 3 chunks of wood or a handful of wood chips, unless the smoker takes dry wood.
3. Fill the fire pan full with charcoal briquettes and start the fire.
4. When the coals turn grey, drain the wood pieces and add them to the coals. (For electric units: unless the smoker takes dry wood, drain the wood pieces and put them in their special pan.)
5. Put the water pan in place and fill it with hot water.
6. Put the cooking grill in place.
7. Lift the ribs from the marinade and arrange them on the cooking grill.
8. Cover. (Plug in electric smoker.) Smoke-cook about 4 hours.

Makes about 4 servings

Tangerine Frozen Yogurt to go with Deviled Beef Ribs

Refreshingly tart, this tangerine-flavored dessert will win praises from kids and adults. You could serve it in cones for the youngsters or layer it with fresh fruit in parfait glasses for grown-ups. Either way it is an excellent conclusion to a Deviled Beef Rib dinner.

½ **envelope unflavored gelatin**
¼ **cup cold water**
1 **cup boiling water**
8 **ounces plain or vanilla yogurt**
⅔ **cup instant nonfat dry milk**
¼ **teaspoon salt**
1 **(6-ounce) can frozen tangerine juice concentrate, partially thawed**

1. In a blender container, combine the gelatin and cold water. Wait 1 minute for the gelatin to soften, then add the boiling water.
2. Cover and blend on high speed until all the gelatin granules are dissolved.
3. Add the yogurt, milk powder, salt and tangerine juice and blend until smooth.
4. Pour the mixture into a shallow metal dish and freeze until slushy.
5. Remove from the freezer and quickly beat smooth.
6. Return to the freezer and freeze firm.
7. Allow the frozen yogurt to soften briefly at room temperature before serving.

Makes 4 to 6 servings

Kids will love to eat Deviled Beef Ribs and adults will appreciate their flavor.

Fantastic Rib Ends

Ask your butcher to bone short ribs for this tasty specialty. Four or five pieces of meat make a full meal. You can also cut smaller portions to serve as appetizers. Fantastic Cole Slaw (see accompanying recipe), Smoker Roasted Corn on The Cob (see "Smoker Side Dishes"), some garlic bread and an assortment of fresh fruit could complete the meal.

About 6 pounds boneless beef short ribs
1 bottle (8 ounces) or 1 cup Russian or Western-style dressing

The Night Before Serving
1. Arrange the ribs in a baking dish, bowl or heavy-duty plastic bag and pour the dressing over them.
2. Stir or toss lightly so each piece of meat gets coated with dressing.
3. Cover with plastic wrap or close the bag securely.
4. Refrigerate overnight.

About 5½ to 6 Hours Before Serving
1. Remove the meat from the refrigerator.
2. Start soaking 2 or 3 chunks of wood or a handful of wood chips, unless the smoker takes dry wood.
3. Fill the fire pan full with charcoal briquettes and start the fire.
4. When the coals turn grey, drain the wood pieces and add them to the coals. (For electric units: unless the smoker takes dry wood, drain the wood pieces and put them in their special pan.)
5. Put the water pan in place and fill with hot water.
6. Put the cooking grill in place.
7. Arrange the pieces of meat on the grill.
8. Cover. (Plug in electric smoker.) Smoke-cook about 5 hours or until the meat is tender. After about 4 hours, you may need to check the water pan and add a quart or so of hot water. Ribs will wait at least an hour in the smoker after they are done.

Makes about 8 to 10 servings

Cole Slaw to go with Fantastic Rib Ends

Tart apples combine with cabbage for a special cole slaw that goes with Fantastic Rib Ends. McIntosh, Cortland or Jonathan apples would be a good choice.

4 to 5 medium-sized apples
3 medium-sized carrots
3 cups shredded cabbage
¾ to 1 cup mayonnaise or combination dairy sour cream and mayonnaise
2 tablespoons lemon juice
1 teaspoon salt
¾ cup raisins (optional)

1. Core and shred the unpeeled apples.
2. Peel and shred the carrots.
3. Combine all the ingredients and mix well.

Makes 8 to 12 servings

Tangy Barbecued Beef

Smoked beef marinated in a spicy barbecue sauce is a double treat; the mellow smoked flavor and the tangy sauce are delicious together. Try the lively marinade on a boneless roast, a thick chuck steak or even a pot roast. To be sure of extra-tender meat, treat a less-tender cut with unseasoned meat tenderizer just before you put it on the cooking grill. The drippings in the water pan will make a superb gravy (see "Gravies, Marinades and Sauces"), so plan to serve a potato or rice dish to show off the gravy. Crisp-cooked vegetables, a simple tomato vinaigrette, plus Tangy Peach Sherbet for dessert could round out your menu.

1 (4-pound) boneless beef roast or round-bone pot roast
⅓ cup red wine vinegar
¼ cup catsup
¼ cup soy sauce
2 tablespoons oil
1 tablespoon Worcestershire sauce
1 teaspoon salt
½ teaspoon dry mustard
¼ teaspoon pepper
1 clove garlic, minced

The Night Before Serving

1. Put the meat in a baking dish or heavy-duty plastic bag.
2. In a small mixing bowl or 1-pint measuring cup, combine all the remaining ingredients.
3. Pour the marinade over the meat. Turn the meat so it is completely coated with marinade.
4. Cover with plastic wrap or close the bag securely.
5. Refrigerate overnight.

About 5½ to 6 Hours Before Serving

1. Remove the meat from the refrigerator.
2. Start soaking 2 or 3 chunks of wood or a handful of wood chips, unless the smoker takes dry wood.
3. Fill the fire pan full with charcoal briquettes and start the fire.
4. When the coals turn grey, drain the wood pieces and add them to the coals. (For electric units: unless the smoker takes dry wood, drain the wood pieces and put them in their special pan.)
5. Put the water pan in place and fill it almost full with hot water.
6. Put the cooking grill in place.
7. Lift the meat from the marinade and put it in the center of the cooking grill. Pour the marinade into the water pan.
8. Cover. (Plug in electric smoker.) Smoke-cook about 5 hours or until the meat is firm to the touch. After about 4 hours, you may need to check the water pan and add a quart or so of hot water.
9. Cut in thin slices to serve.

Makes 6 to 8 servings

Peach Sherbet to go with Tangy Barbecued Beef

Sherbets were served at Edwardian banquets to "refresh the palate" between courses. After you have enjoyed the richly seasoned Tangy Barbecued Beef, tangy Peach Sherbet may be just the dessert to refresh your palate. Peach brandy adds a sophisticated touch to the sherbet.

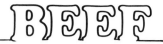

Peach Sherbet to go with Tangy Barbecued Beef (continued)

3 tablespoons peach brandy
1 envelope unflavored gelatin
1 (16-ounce) can juice-packed peaches, drained, reserving juice
¼ teaspoon salt or butter-flavored salt

1. Pour the brandy into a blender container.
2. Sprinkle in the gelatin and wait 1 minute until the granules soften.
3. Measure the peach juice and add cold water if necessary to equal 1½ cups. Heat the juice and water to boiling.
4. Pour the juice into the blender, cover, and blend until all the gelatin granules are dissolved.
5. Add the peaches and salt; cover and blend until smooth.
6. Pour the mixture into a shallow metal dish and freeze only until slushy.
7. Break up the sherbet into a mixing bowl and beat until fluffy.
8. Pour the sherbet back into the shallow metal dish and freeze until firm.
9. Soften briefly before serving.

Makes 8 servings

Tangy Barbecued Beef is an appealing main course accompanied by crisp-cooked vegetables.

BEEF

Dilly Short Ribs

Dill-flavored ribs suggests a Scandanavian menu, dill being an herb much appreciated in those Northern countries. You could start with a refreshing fruit soup and then serve the short ribs with boiled new potatoes and gravy made from the delicious drippings in the water pan (see "Gravies, Marinades and Sauces"). Set out a small smorgasbord of condiments such as Pickled Mushrooms, as well as fresh vegetables and fruits to contrast with the ribs and potatoes.

5 to 6 pound beef short ribs
½ cup oil
⅓ cup red wine, cider or white vinegar
2 tablespoons mustard sauce
1 teaspoon onion salt
1 teaspoon dried dill weed
⅛ teaspoon hot pepper sauce

The Night Before Serving
1. Arrange the ribs in a baking dish, bowl or heavy-duty plastic bag.
2. In a small bowl or measuring cup, combine all the remaining ingredients and blend.
3. Pour the marinade over the ribs. Turn the ribs to coat them completely with the marinade.
4. Cover with plastic wrap or close the bag securely.
5. Refrigerate at least several hours, preferably overnight, turning occasionally.

About 6 Hours Before Serving
1. Remove the meat from the refrigerator.
2. Start soaking 2 or 3 chunks of wood or a handful of wood chips, unless the smoker takes dry wood.
3. Fill the fire pan full with charcoal briquettes and start the fire.
4. When the coals turn grey, drain the wood pieces and add them to the coals. (For electric units: unless the smoker takes dry wood, drain the wood pieces and put them in their special pan.)
5. Put the water pan in place and fill it with hot water.
6. Put the cooking grill in place.
7. Lift the ribs from the marinade and put them on the cooking grill.
8. Pour the marinade over the meat and into the water pan.
9. Cover. (Plug in electric smoker.) Smoke-cook about 5 hours or until the meat is tender. After about 4 hours, you may need to check the water pan and add a quart or so of hot water.

Makes about 6 servings

Pickled Mushrooms to go with Dilly Short Ribs

Contrast in taste and texture makes a meal interesting. Fresh mushrooms and onion slices marinated in tarragon vinegar are delightful, tart contrasts to Dilly Short Ribs. The mushrooms should marinate in the refrigerator for 24 hours before serving.

Pickled Mushrooms to go with Dilly Short Ribs (continued)

1 medium onion
4 cups tiny fresh
   mushrooms
¾ cup tarragon vinegar
¼ cup water
3 tablespoons corn or
   safflower oil
1 garlic clove, minced
1½ teaspoons salt
¼ teaspoon pepper
⅛ teaspoon cayenne pepper

1. Peel the onion and slice it in rings.
2. Clean the mushrooms and trim the ends, if necessary.
3. Combine all the ingredients in a bowl.
4. Cover and refrigerate 24 hours.
5. Drain before serving.

Makes 6 to 8 servings

Bloody Mary Pot Roast

Named after the drink, the spicy, flavorful marinade in this recipe gives everyday pot roast a sophisticated sparkle. You can also use the marinade for a boneless beef or pork roast. The versatile marinade even can be simmered in a saucepan for a few minutes to develop flavors and used as a brush-on barbecue sauce.

1 (3- to 4-pound) beef pot
   roast
1½ cups tomato juice or
   vegetable cocktail juice
½ cup finely chopped onion
½ cup finely chopped green
   pepper
¼ cup red wine vinegar
¼ to ½ cup vodka
   (optional)
¼ to ½ teaspoon red pepper
   flakes or generous dash
   hot pepper sauce
1 teaspoon salt
1 teaspoon Worcestershire
   sauce
½ teaspoon basil
1 clove garlic, minced

The Night Before Serving

1. Put the pot roast in a glass baking dish or heavy-duty plastic bag.
2. Combine all the remaining ingredients in a small mixing bowl and mix well to make the marinade.
3. Pour the marinade over the roast. Turn the roast and spoon the marinade over it so all surfaces are covered.
4. Cover with plastic wrap or close the bag securely.
5. Refrigerate overnight. Turn the meat in the marinade once or twice, if you think of it.

About 5 Hours Before Serving

1. Remove the meat from the refrigerator.
2. Start soaking 2 or 3 chunks of wood or a handful of wood chips, unless the smoker takes dry wood.
3. Fill the fire pan full with charcoal briquettes and start the fire.
4. When the coals turn grey, drain the wood pieces and add them to the coals. (For electric units: unless the smoker takes dry wood, drain the wood pieces and put them in their special pan.)
5. Put the water pan in place and fill almost full with hot water.
6. Put the cooking grill in place.
7. Lift the meat from the marinade and put it in the center of the cooking grill. Pour the marinade into the water pan.
8. Cover. (Plug in electric smoker.) Smoke-cook about 4 to 5 hours or until the meat feels firm to the touch. After about 4 hours, you may need to check the water pan and add a quart or so of hot water.
9. Cut the meat in thin slices to serve.

Makes 4 to 6 servings

BEEF

Savory Eggplant to go with Bloody Mary Pot Roast

This vegetable dish tastes twice as rich as it is — rather like an extravagant Mediterranean version of hot potato salad. Served with Bloody Mary Pot Roast and Herbed Smoked Tomatoes (see "Smoker Side Dishes") this vegetable dish will make your dinner extra special.

2 **large potatoes, peeled**
⅓ **pound bacon, cut in 1-inch pieces**
2 **medium onions, peeled**
1 **clove garlic**
3 **cups peeled, cubed eggplant**
¼ **cup olive oil or cooking oil**
4 **tablespoons tarragon vinegar**
1½ **tablespoons Dijon mustard**
3 **tablespoons grated Parmesan cheese**
1 **teaspoon salt**
¼ **teaspoon pepper**

1. Quarter the potatoes and cook them in boiling salted water to cover until just tender.
2. Coarsely chop the potatoes. Set them aside.
3. Cook the bacon pieces in a large skillet until crisp. Remove the bacon, reserving the drippings in the skillet.
4. Slice the onion and garlic.
5. Sauté the onion, garlic and eggplant in the bacon drippings and oil until tender.
6. Gently stir in the potatoes.
7. Blend the vinegar and mustard. Sprinkle them over the potato mixture, along with the Parmesan cheese, salt and pepper.

Makes 6 servings

Smoked Corned Beef

Impossible to get tender, juicy corned beef without simmering, you say? Not impossible, if you use one of the new specially tenderized corned beef briskets for oven smoking. The leftovers are great for Smoked Reuben Sandwiches!

1 **(2½- to 3½-pound) corned beef brisket for oven roasting**

About 7½ Hours Before Serving
1. Tear off an 18-inch piece of heavy-duty foil. Fold up the edges slightly.
2. Open the pouch of corned beef brisket and put the brisket in the center of the foil. Pour the juices from the pouch over the brisket. Bring up sides of foil to form a pan around the brisket.
3. Start soaking 2 or 3 chunks of wood or a handful of wood chips, unless the smoker takes dry wood.
4. Fill the fire pan full of charcoal briquettes and start the fire.
5. When the coals turn grey, drain the wood pieces and add them to coals. (For electric units: unless the smoker takes dry wood, drain the wood pieces and add them to their special pan.)
6. Put the water pan in place and fill almost full with hot water.
7. Put the cooking grill in place.
8. Put the foil tray and brisket in the center of the cooking grill.
9. Cover. (Plug in electric smoker.) Smoke-cook about 6½ to 7 hours. After about 4 hours you may need to check the water pan and add a quart or so of hot water.

Makes 6 to 8 servings

Smoked Reuben Sandwiches made with Smoked Corned Beef

The original Reuben was the winner of a sandwich idea contest back in 1956. Using leftover smoked corned beef, you will have a champion sandwich of your own. Don't forget to serve these hearty sandwiches with big, juicy dill pickles.

12 slices rye bread
½ cup Thousand Island
   dressing
6 slices Swiss cheese
⅔ cup drained sauerkraut
½ pound thin-sliced
   smoked corned beef
   Butter or margarine,
   softened

1. Spread 6 of the bread slices with dressing.
2. Place a slice of cheese on top of each piece of "dressed" bread.
3. Place about 2 tablespoons of kraut on each cheese slice and put the smoked corned beef on top of the kraut.
4. Close the sandwiches with the remaining bread slices.
5. Spread the outsides of the sandwiches with butter and grill them until browned.

Makes 6 servings

Smoked Meat Loaf

An easy and economical feast! Put some new potatoes in the water pan to cook along with the meat loaf. You can also wrap sliced zucchini, Italian green beans or any other green vegetable in foil to tuck on the cooking grill along with the meat loaf. Served with Fresh Tomato Aspic, an everyday meatloaf meal turns into a festive dinner.

3 pounds ground beef or 2
   pounds ground beef and
   1 pound ground pork
3 eggs
1 can (8 ounces) tomato
   sauce
3 tablespoons prepared
   mustard
3 tablespoons molasses
2 tablespoons instant
   minced onion
2 tablespoons dehydrated
   pepper flakes or ¼ cup
   finely chopped green
   pepper
½ cup oatmeal
1 teaspoon salt

About 5 to 6 Hours Before Serving

1. Combine all the ingredients in a large mixing bowl and mix well with your hands or a wooden spoon.
2. Tear off a sheet of heavy-duty foil about 20 inches long.
3. Turn the meat mixture out of the bowl onto the foil and shape it into a loaf.
4. Fold the edges of the foil over and over until they meet the edge of the loaf and form a shallow pan.
5. Start soaking 2 or 3 chunks of wood or a handful of wood chips, unless the smoker takes dry wood.
6. Fill the fire pan full with charcoal briquettes and start the fire.
7. When the coals turn grey, drain the wood pieces and add them to the coals. (For electric units: unless the smoker takes dry wood, drain the wood pieces and put them in their special pan.)
8. Put the water pan in place and fill it with hot water.
9. Put the cooking grill in place.
10. Place the meat loaf in its foil pan in the center of the cooking grill.
11. Cover. (Plug in electric smoker.) Smoke-cook about 5 hours or until the center of the loaf feels firm to the touch. After about 4 hours, you may need to check the water pan and add a quart or so of hot water. An extra hour in the cooker will not overcook the meat loaf.

Makes about 8 servings

Fresh Tomato Aspic for Smoked Meat Loaf

When you use fresh tomatoes, the classic tomato aspic recipe almost turns into molded gazpacho. If you like, you could garnish the salad with avocado, and green pepper slices.

4 large tomatoes, halved and seeded
1 small onion, peeled and quartered
3 stalks celery
1 tablespoon sugar
1 teaspoon salt
1 bay leaf
2 envelopes unflavored gelatin
½ cup cold water
3 tablespoons vinegar
2 tablespoons lemon juice
½ teaspoon Worcestershire sauce
Crisp salad greens

1. Finely chop the tomatoes, onion and celery.
2. Place the tomato mixture, sugar, salt and bay leaf in a medium-sized saucepan; simmer 30 minutes.
3. Sprinkle the gelatin over cold water in a large bowl; wait one minute for the granules to soften.
4. Pour the hot tomato mixture over the gelatin. Blend until the gelatin is dissolved. Add the vinegar, lemon juice and Worcestershire sauce. Remove the bay leaf.
5. Measure the mixture and add enough water to make 4 cups. Pour the aspic into a 4-cup mold.
6. Chill until firm. Unmold the salad onto crisp salad greens.

Makes about 8 servings

Mama's Brisket is especially tender when cut across the grain in thin slices.

Mama's Brisket

Well, it's not exactly Mama's, because she did hers in a big pot on the stove. This one goes outside, in the smoke cooker, and tastes like Mama's, only better. Be sure to cut thin slices, at a slant, across the grain of the meat.

1 (5-pound) beef brisket
1 envelope dry onion soup mix
1 tablespoon water

About 7 Hours Before Serving

1. Remove the meat from the refrigerator and let it stand while preparing the fire.
2. Start soaking 2 or 3 chunks of wood or a handful of wood chips, unless the smoker takes dry wood.
3. Fill the fire pan full with charcoal briquettes and start the fire.
4. When the coals turn grey, drain the wood pieces and add them to the coals. (For electric units: unless the smoker takes dry wood, drain the wood pieces and put them in their special pan.)
5. Put the water pan in place and fill almost full with hot water.
6. Put the cooking grill in place.
7. Combine the soup mix and water and stir. Spread over the top of the brisket.
8. Put the brisket in the center of the cooking grill.
9. Cover. (Plug in electric smoker.) Smoke-cook about 6½ hours. After about 4 hours, you may need to check the water pan and add a quart or so of water.

Makes about 10 servings

Blueberry Dumpling Dessert to go with Mama's Brisket

Sometimes called Blueberry Slump or Blueberry Grunt, this not-too-sweet dessert is an old-fashioned ending for a smoke-cooked meal. See the chapter on "Smoker Side Dishes" for Garden on the Grill, and perhaps include a tossed salad to complete a delicious menu. The dumpling dessert can be served with cream, whipped cream or ice cream, if you want.

Blueberry "filling"

1½ pints (3 cups) fresh blueberries, washed and drained
½ cup sugar
1 cup water
⅛ teaspoon salt
1 tablespoon lemon juice
½ teaspoon cinnamon (optional)

Dumpling topping

1 cup enriched all-purpose flour
2 tablespoons sugar
2 teaspoons baking powder
½ teaspoon salt
2 tablespoons butter
½ cup milk

1. In a large skillet or saucepan that has a cover, mix the blueberries with the sugar, water and salt, lemon juice and cinnamon. Heat to boiling.
2. Lower the heat, cover and simmer 5 minutes.
3. Meanwhile, prepare the dumpling topping by stirring together the flour, sugar, baking powder and salt. Cut in the butter until the particles are very small.
4. Stir the milk into the dry ingredients and mix just until moistened.
5. Drop 8 spoonfuls of dough onto the bubbling fruit, arranging the dumplings so they do not touch each other.
6. Cover tightly and simmer 10 minutes.
7. Serve hot or warm.

Makes 8 to 10 servings

California Beef Kababs

If you like skewered vegetables along with Kababs, string some green pepper, tomato and onion chunks, along with whole mushroom caps, and put them on the cooking grill for the last hour of cooking time. Brush with oil or melted butter before and after you put them in the smoke cooker.

2 pounds lean boneless beef (such as top round or sirloin tip) cut into 1½-inch chunks
1 envelope onion soup mix
⅔ cup oil
¼ cup cider vinegar or lemon juice

The Night Before Serving
1. Combine all the ingredients in a heavy-duty plastic bag or deep glass bowl. Stir to coat the beef chunks.
2. Close the bag or cover the bowl with plastic wrap and refrigerate overnight.

About 4 Hours Before Serving
1. Remove the meat from the refrigerator and let it stand while preparing the fire.
2. Start soaking 2 or 3 chunks of wood or a handful or wood chips, unless the smoker takes dry wood.
3. Fill the fire pan full with charcoal briquettes and start the fire.
4. When the coals turn grey, drain the wood pieces and add them to the coals. (For electric units: unless the smoker takes dry wood, drain the wood pieces and put them in their special pan.)
5. Put the water pan in place and fill almost full with hot water.
6. Put the cooking grill in place.
7. Put the chunks of beef on skewers. Place the skewers on the cooking grill. Pour any leftover marinade into the water pan.
8. Cover. (Plug in electric smoker.) Smoke-cook about 3 to 3½ hours.

Makes 6 to 8 servings

Cantaloupe Freeze to go with California Beef Kababs

A cool, refreshing conclusion to California Beef Kababs, West Coast Cantaloupe Freeze is a dressed-up variation on vanilla ice cream in a cantaloupe. It also resembles baked Alaska, being covered with meringue and baked for a few minutes.

4 small cantaloupes
2 cups sliced strawberries
4 tablespoons sugar
2 pints lemon, orange, pineapple or strawberry sherbet or vanilla ice cream

Meringue
6 egg whites
¼ teaspoon salt
⅔ cup sugar

1. Cut the cantaloupes in half and scoop out the seeds.
2. Divide the strawberries among the cantaloupe halves.
3. Sprinkle with sugar.
4. Put a dip of sherbet or ice cream in each melon half and put the filled halves in the freezer.
5. Preheat the oven to 450°F.
6. Beat the egg whites with the salt until foamy.
7. Gradually add the sugar and beat to stiff peaks.
8. Remove the cantaloupe halves from the freezer and spread the meringue over the ice cream, sealing to the edge of the cantaloupe halves.
9. Put the halves on baking sheets and bake for 3 to 5 minutes or until meringue is golden.
10. Serve at once.

Makes 8 servings

LAMB

Besides the impressive Herbed Leg of Lamb, stuffed with a delightful combination of minced parsley, garlic and rosemary, you can enjoy smoke-cooked recipes for lamb chops, lamb shanks, lamb ribs and skewered lamb. All of them will fill the air with the irresistible aroma of herbs and spices, whetting the appetite for good dining with good friends.

Herbed Leg of Lamb

Fit for a banquet, Herbed Leg of Lamb could be served with Fruited Rice (see "Smoker Side Dishes"), a crunchy cole slaw, French bread and fresh fruit for a superb menu. Tucking a mixture of chopped vegetables and herbs into little pockets in the meat adds extra flavor. Use a meat thermometer to help you accurately gauge when the lamb is done — 160°F is the temperature for medium, 170°F for well done.

1 **(5-pound) leg of lamb**
1 **medium onion, minced**
1 **handful parsley springs, minced**
2 **cloves garlic, minced**
1 **teaspoon rosemary, crushed**
1 **teaspoon salt**
½ **teaspoon pepper or lemon pepper**

About 6 Hours Before Serving

1. Remove the meat from the refrigerator.
2. Combine all the remaining ingredients.
3. With the tip of a very sharp knife, make several cuts straight-down into meat. Space the cuts several inches apart all over surface of meat. The cuts should be an inch or two deep.
4. Using the tip of a knife, spoon or finger, stuff the onion mixture into the cuts. Spread any remaining onion mixture over surface of meat. Insert the meat thermometer with tip in center of largest muscle, away from bone or fat.
5. Start soaking 2 or 3 chunks of wood or a handful of wood chips unless the smoker takes dry wood.
6. Fill the fire pan full of charcoal briquettes and start the fire.
7. When the coals turn grey, drain the wood pieces and add them to the coals. (For electric units: unless the smoker takes dry wood, drain the wood pieces and put them in their special pan.)
8. Put the water pan in place and fill almost full with hot water.
9. Set the cooking grill in place.
10. Place the meat on the cooking grill.
11. Cover. (Plug in electric unit.) Smoke-cook about 5 to 5½ hours or until the lamb is done to your taste. The thermometer should register 160°F for medium, 170°F for well done.

Makes about 8 servings

A gourmet's treat, Herbed Leg of Lamb starts with minced onions, parsley, garlic and crushed rosemary — all traditional seasonings for Lamb. You could use a blender or food processor to do the mincing, or do it by hand.

Use a very sharp knife to make several cuts straight down into the meat. Make the cuts an inch or two deep.

Stuff the minced onion and herb mixture into the cuts. You can use your finger or the top of a knife or spoon to insert the stuffing. Leftover stuffing can be spread on top of the lamb.

Put a meat thermometer in the thickest part of the meat. Make sure the tip does not touch the bone. When the smoker is ready, place the leg of lamb in the center of the grill.

Smoke-cook the lamb for 5 to 5½ hours. The thermometer should read 160°F for medium, 170°F for well done.

Wearing oven mitts, remove the leg of lamb from the grill.

Herbed Leg of Lamb, Fruited Rice and cole slaw are ready for a banquet.

Armenian Lamb Kababs

Serve these savory kababs with rice pilaf, sliced cucumbers in yogurt, hot pita bread and fresh fruit for dessert — a sumptuous feast! You will need 6 skewers.

2 pounds lean boneless lamb, cut in 1½-inch chunks
¼ cup lemon juice
¼ cup sherry
1 teaspoon rosemary, crushed
1 clove garlic, minced

About 6 to 8 Hours Before Serving

1. Combine all the ingredients in a heavy-duty plastic bag or deep glass bowl. Stir to coat the lamb chunks.
2. Close the bag securely or cover the bowl with plastic wrap and refrigerate for several hours.

About 3 Hours Before Serving

1. Start soaking 2 or 3 chunks of wood or a handful of wood chips, unless the smoker takes dry wood.
2. Remove the meat from the refrigerator and let stand while preparing the fire.
3. Fill the fire pan full of charcoal briquettes and start the fire.
4. When the coals turn grey, drain the wood and add them to the coals. (For electric units: unless the smoker takes dry wood, drain the wood pieces and put them in their special pan.)
5. Put the water pan in place and fill almost full with water.
6. Set the cooking grill in place.
7. Put the chunks of lamb on skewers. Place the skewers on the cooking grill. Pour any leftover marinade into the water pan.
8. Cover. (Plug in electric smoker.) Smoke-cook about 2½ hours.

Makes 6 servings

Rice Pilaf to go with Armenian Lamb Kababs

A fancy rice dish, this pilaf complements Armenian Lamb Kababs with the addition of chopped dried apricots and toasted nuts. Herbed Smoked Tomatoes from the "Smoker Side Dishes" chapter could be another distinctive addition to your Near-East banquet.

2 tablespoons butter
½ cup chopped onion
1½ cups rice
4 cups chicken broth
½ teaspoon salt
1½ teaspoons cumin (optional)
¼ cup chopped parsley
½ cup chopped dried apricots
⅓ cup pine nuts, chopped walnuts or slivered almonds

1. Heat the butter in large frying pan and sauté the onion over medium heat until it is limp.
2. Add the rice and sauté over low heat for about 4 minutes, or until the rice is golden.
3. In a large saucepan, heat the broth to boiling.
4. Add the salt, cumin, parsley, apricots and sautéed rice mixture to the broth.
5. Cover and simmer for 25 minutes, or until the rice is fluffy.
6. While the rice cooks, toast the nuts in a 325° F oven for 8 to 10 minutes, or until light brown.
7. Sprinkle nuts over the rice before serving.

Makes 6 to 8 servings

Curried Lamb on Skewers

The curry flavor is mild and subtle in this recipe. If you prefer a stronger curry taste, use 2 teaspoons of curry powder. Serve these tender, robust cubes of lamb with rice, a crisp green salad and fruit sherbet to make an outdoor meal with a difference. You will need 6 skewers.

2 pounds lean boneless lamb or beef, cut in 1½-inch chunks
¼ cup oil
¼ cup cider vinegar
1 tablespoon instant minced onion
1 teaspoon curry powder, or more
½ teaspoon salt
1 clove garlic, minced

The Night Before Serving
1. Combine all ingredients in heavy-duty plastic bag or deep glass bowl. Stir to coat the lamb chunks.
2. Cover with plastic wrap or close the bag securely and refrigerate overnight.

About 3 Hours Before Serving
1. Start soaking 2 or 3 chunks of wood or a handful of wood chips, unless the smoker takes dry wood.
2. Remove the meat from the refrigerator and let it stand while preparing the fire.
3. Fill the fire pan full of charcoal briquettes and start the fire.
4. When the coals turn grey, drain the wood pieces and add them to the coals. (For electric units: unless the smoker takes dry wood, drain the wood pieces and put them in their special pan.)
5. Put the water pan in place and fill almost full with hot water.
6. Set the cooking grill in place.
7. Put the chunks of meat on skewers. Arrange them on the cooking grill. Pour any leftover marinade into the water pan.
8. Cover. (Plug in electric smoker.) Smoke-cook about 2½ hours.

Makes about 6 servings

Fresh Lemon–Lime Sherbet to go with Curried Lamb on Skewers

A zesty citrus sherbet ends a curried lamb dinner on a light note. You can prepare the sherbet several days in advance, if you want. Serve the sherbet plain or with a combination of honeydew and cantaloupe melon balls. You could use all lemons or all limes in this recipe.

4 lemons
4 limes
1 cup sugar
2 cups milk
3 or 4 drops green food coloring (optional)
2 egg whites
2 tablespoons sugar
1 cup whipping cream

1. Grate the thin, outer colored portion of the peel from the lemons and limes.
2. Mix the grated peel with the cup of sugar in a blender.
3. Squeeze the juice from the lemons and limes.
4. Add the milk, citrus juice and green food coloring (optional) to the lime peel and sugar mixture. Blend until smooth.
5. Pour the mixture into ice cube trays or a shallow metal pan. Freeze until firm, about 1½ hours.
6. Beat the egg whites with a mixer until frothy. Gradually add 2 tablespoons sugar and beat until stiff.
7. Whip the cream with a mixer until it is thick but not stiff.
8. Break the frozen mixture into chunks and beat in a blender until smooth.
9. Fold in the whipped cream and egg whites.
10. Spoon into 8 serving dishes or glasses. Place them in the freezer compartment. Freeze until firm, about 2 hours.

Makes 8 servings

Lively Lamb Chops

Select lamb shoulder chops or steaks cut from the leg for this delicious version of lamb chops. The marinade is the ultimate in simplicity — a bottled dressing.

6 **(3/4-inch thick) lamb shoulder chops or steaks**
1 **cup bottled garlic or Italian salad dressing**

The Night Before Serving

1. Place the chops in a baking dish or heavy-duty plastic bag.
2. Pour the dressing over the chops, turning the chops so they are completely coated.
3. Cover with plastic wrap or close the bag securely and refrigerate overnight, turning occasionally.

About 4½ Hours Before Serving

1. Remove the lamb from the refrigerator.
2. Start soaking 2 or 3 chunks of wood or a handful of wood chips, unless the smoker takes dry wood.
3. Fill the fire pan full of charcoal briquettes and start the fire.
4. When the coals turn grey, drain the wood pieces and add them to the coals. (For electric units: unless the smoker takes dry wood, drain the wood pieces and add them to their special pan.)
5. Set the water pan in place and fill almost full with hot water.
6. Put the cooking grill in place.
7. Lift the lamb chops from the marinade and arrange them on the cooking grill.
8. Pour the marinade over lamb, letting the excess run into the water pan.
9. Cover. (Plug in electric smoker.) Smoke-cook about 4 hours.

Makes 6 servings

Citrus Squash Cook–Along to go with Lively Lamb Chops

A fancy version of baked squash, Citrus Acorn Squash can cook along with the chops if your grill is large enough, or if you have a double grill. To prepare the squash in an oven, put the squash, cavity side down, in a baking pan with 1 inch of hot water. Bake the squash at 375°F for 30 or 40 minutes. Then, prepare the filling as directed and return the squash halves to the oven for 5 to 10 minutes. Buttered noodles and a salad of romaine, green pepper and green onions also would be good complements to Lively Lamb Chops.

3 **medium acorn squash**
2 **tablespoons brown sugar**
2 **teaspoons cornstarch**
½ **cup fresh tangerine or orange juice, strained**
1 **teaspoon grated lemon peel**
1 **tablespoon lemon juice**
1 **tablespoon butter**
¼ **teaspoon salt**
½ **teaspoon nutmeg**
4 **tangerines, peeled, seeded and sectioned**
Dash salt and pepper

About 3½ Hours Before Serving

1. Cut the squash in half and scoop out the seeds and strings.
2. Put the squash, cavity side down, on the smoker's grill and smoke-cook about 3 hours or until squash is tender
3. Meanwhile, blend the sugar and cornstarch in a saucepan.
4. Stir in the tangerine or orange juice.
5. Cook and stir over medium heat until the mixture comes to a boil and is smooth and thickened.
6. Stir in the lemon peel, juice, butter, salt and nutmeg until the butter melts. Stir in the tangerine sections.
7. Sprinkle the cavities of the squash with additional salt and pepper, then spoon in the tangerine mixture.
8. Return the squash to the smoker for about 30 minutes to heat through.

Makes 6 servings

Citrus–Sherry Lamb Ribs

A relatively inexpensive cut of lamb, the ribs take well to marinating and smoke-cooking. If you have a special rib rack for your smoke cooker, here's the place to use it. You also can use breast of lamb for this recipe. Stick some sweet potatoes on the special spikes at the side of the rib rack for the last 2 hours of cooking. If you do not have a rib rack you may want to cut the slabs of ribs into smaller portions so you fit it all on the cooking grill.

4 to 5 pounds lamb riblets or breast
1 cup orange juice
½ cup sherry
¼ cup honey
3 tablespoons cider vinegar
3 tablespoons chopped parsley or 1 tablespoon chopped chives
1 teaspoon salt

The Night Before Serving

1. Cut the ribs into small portions, if you wish. Place the portions or slabs of ribs in a baking dish or heavy-duty plastic bag.
2. Combine orange juice, sherry, honey, vinegar, parsley and salt in small mixing bowl. Mix until the honey blends in to make a marinade.
3. Pour the marinade over ribs. Toss and turn the ribs so each piece is coated.
4. Cover with plastic wrap or close the bag securely.
5. Refrigerate overnight.

About 5 to 6 Hours Before Serving

1. Remove the meat from the refrigerator.
2. Start soaking 2 or 3 chunks of wood or a handful of wood chips, unless the smoker takes dry wood.
3. Fill the fire pan full of charcoal briquettes and start the fire.
4. When the coals turn grey, drain the wood pieces and add them to the coals. (For electric units: unless the smoker takes dry wood, drain the wood pieces and put them in their special pan.)
5. Set the water pan in place and fill with hot water.
6. Put the cooking grill in place.
7. Arrange the ribs in the rib holder or on the cooking grill.
8. Cover. (Plug in electric smoker.) Smoke-cook about 4½ to 5 hours or until meat is well browned and tender. After about 4 hours, you may need to check the water pan and add a quart or so of hot water. The ribs will wait at least an hour in the cooker after they are done.

Makes 4 to 6 servings

Salad Tangiers to go with Citrus–Sherry Lamb Ribs

The perfect companion to Citrus-Sherry Lamb Ribs, cumin is the main spice in this spunky salad. Be sure to make the salad several hours ahead of time so it can chill thoroughly and the vegetables can soak up the marvelously tart dressing.

Salad Tangiers to go with Citrus–Sherry Lamb Ribs (continued)

Dressing

1 tablespoon olive oil
3 tablespoons garlic-flavored red wine vinegar
2 teaspoons ground cumin
3 tablespoons dry red wine
1 teaspoon salt
1 teaspoon pepper
1 tablespoon chopped parsley

Salad

1 small onion
2 large green peppers
2 medium tomatoes

1. Combine the oil, vinegar, cumin, wine, salt, pepper and parsley in a bowl.
2. Peel and thinly slice the onion.
3. Seed and cut the green peppers into bite-sized chunks.
4. Peel and cube the tomatoes.
5. Add all the vegetables to the dressing.
6. Toss the mixture well.
7. Refrigerate it until thoroughly chilled.

Makes 6 servings

Garlicky Lamb Shanks

You could use almost any salad dressing mix for the marinade — blue cheese, green goddess or French. Or, you could use your own French or garlic dressing to give the lamb shanks a zippy flavor.

4 to 6 lamb shanks
1 envelope garlic salad dressing mix
3/4 cup oil
½ cup red wine vinegar

The Night Before Serving

1. Put the lamb shanks in a deep glass bowl or heavy-duty plastic bag.
2. Combine all remaining ingredients in small bowl. Pour over the lamb shanks.
3. Cover with plastic wrap or close the bag and refrigerate overnight.

About 5 Hours Before Serving

1. Remove the lamb from the refrigerator.
2. Start soaking 2 or 3 chunks of wood or a handful of wood chips, unless the smoker takes dry wood.
3. Fill the fire pan full of charcoal briquettes and start the fire.
4. When the coals turn grey, drain the wood pieces and add them to the coals. (For electric units: unless the smoker takes dry wood, drain the wood pieces and put them in their special pan.)
5. Put the water pan in place and fill almost full with hot water.
6. Set the cooking grill in place.
7. Arrange the lamb shanks on the cooking grill. Pour the marinade into the water pan.
8. Cover. (Plug in electric smoker.) Smoke-cook about 4 to 5 hours. After about 4 hours you may need to check the water pan and add a quart or so of hot water.

Makes 4 to 6 servings

Garlicky Lamb Shanks make a memorable dinner.

Butterflied Leg of Lamb

It is a good idea to put in an order for a butterflied leg of lamb in advance, then you won't have to wait while the butcher bones it. This tender, boneless cut is easier to carve than a whole leg of lamb.

1 (5- to 6-pound) leg of
    lamb, butterflied
1 can (6 ounces) frozen
    limeade concentrate,
    thawed
1/3 cup white wine vinegar
1 teaspoon rosemary,
    crushed

The Night Before Serving
1. Place the lamb in a deep glass bowl, baking dish or heavy-duty plastic bag.
2. Combine all the ingredients in a small bowl and pour the marinade over the lamb. Turn the lamb in the marinade.
3. Cover with plastic wrap or close the bag securely and refrigerate overnight, turning occasionally.

About 6 Hours Before Serving
1. Remove the meat from the refrigerator.
2. Start soaking 2 or 3 chunks of wood or a handful or two of wood chips, unless the smoker takes dry wood.
3. Fill the fire pan full of charcoal briquettes and start the fire.
4. When the coals turn grey, drain the wood pieces and add them to the coals. (For electric units: unless the smoker takes dry wood, drain the wood pieces and add them to their special pan.)
5. Put the water pan in place and fill almost full with hot water.
6. Set the cooking grill in place.
7. Lift the lamb from the marinade and arrange flat in the center of the cooking grill.
8. Pour the marinade over the lamb, letting the excess run into the water pan.
9. Cover. (Plug in electric smoker.) Smoke-cook about 5 to 5 1/2 hours. After about 4 hours you may need to check the water pan and add a quart or so of hot water.

Makes about 8 servings

Syrian Salad to go with Butterflied Leg of Lamb

Syrian Salad with its snappy dressing contrasts deliciously with Butterflied Leg of Lamb. For a sophisticated dinner cook Fruited Rice (see "Smoker Side Dishes") along with the lamb on the grill and serve an elegantly simple combination of strawberries in champagne for dessert. Syrian Salad could be made with leftover julienne slices of smoked lamb for a luncheon entrée.

1/4 cup olive oil
1/4 cup dry red wine
1/4 cup lemon juice
1 teaspoon garlic salt
1/4 teaspoon pepper
2 teaspoons crushed mint
3 cucumbers, diced
8 black olives, sliced
4 cups shredded spinach
2 medium tomatoes, sliced
1 red onion, sliced in rings

1. Combine the oil, wine, lemon juice, garlic salt, pepper and mint in a medium-sized mixing bowl or glass measuring cup.
2. Add the diced cucumbers and sliced olives to the dressing and let them marinate while you prepare the rest of the salad.
3. In a large salad bowl, arrange the remaining ingredients.
4. Pour the dressing over the salad and toss lightly before serving.

Makes about 8 servings

PORK

PORK

Pork makes an international tour in this chapter: Shanghai Spareribs, Bavarian Pork Roast, Ribs the Island Way, Hawaiian Ham Slices, Hong Kong Pork Chops. But the American way with pork is honored, too. Down South Barbecued Ribs, Lemon-Thyme Country Ribs and McIntosh Pork Chops could carry away prizes in any international competition.

McIntosh Pork Chops

Pork and apples make a superb combination. These chops are soaked in apple juice before being smoke-cooked with apple slices on top.

6 (2-inch thick) pork chops
1 cup apple juice or cider
½ teaspoon pumpkin pie spice, cinnamon or ground cloves
1 or 2 baking apples, sliced

About 6 to 7 Hours Before Serving

1. Arrange the chops in a baking dish.
2. Pour the apple juice over the chops and sprinkle with the spice. Arrange the apple slices on top of the chops.
3. Cover with plastic wrap and refrigerate about 1 hour.
4. Start soaking 2 or 3 chunks of wood or a handful of wood chips, unless the smoker takes dry wood.
5. Fill the fire pan full of charcoal briquettes and start the fire.
6. Remove the chops from the refrigerator.
7. When coals turn grey, drain the wood pieces and add them to the coals. (For electric units: unless the smoker takes dry wood, drain the wood pieces and add them to their special pan.)
8. Set the water pan in place and fill almost full with hot water.
9. Put the cooking grill in place.
10. Place the chops on the cooking grill and pour the marinade into the water pan.
11. Cover. (Plug in electric smoker.) Smoke-cook about 4 to 5 hours. After about 4 hours you may need to check the water pan and add a quart or so of hot water.

Note: Use several 3- or 4-inch lengths of green apple wood for smoking, if you like.

Makes 4 to 6 servings

Apple juice, apples and spice give thick-cut pork chops a delicious tang.

Pour juice over the chops and sprinkle with spice. Slice the apples crosswise to reveal the "star" in the center. Top each chop with an apple slice. Cover and refrigerate about an hour.

Place the chops on the cooking grill, leaving a little space between them. Pour the extra marinade over the chops and into the water pan.

PORK

Figure on smoke-cooking for 4 to 5 hours. The meat is done when it pulls away from the bone easily.

An invitation to fine dining, McIntosh Pork Chops make a succulent entrée.

Ribs the Island Way

Pineapple is a perfect companion to ribs. You can put pineapple slices on the grill for the last few minutes of cooking. Add the savory marinade to the water pan, or save it to simmer and pass as a sauce. You could serve sliced zucchini and yellow squash along with the ribs, then add a pretty green salad, a rice dish some exotic fruits and a nut bread to enjoy an easy luau.

4 pounds spareribs
1 can (8 ounces) crushed pineapple in juice
2 tablespoons honey or brown sugar
2 tablespoons cider vinegar
2 tablespoons minced onion
2 tablespoons minced green pepper
1 teaspoon salt
½ teaspoon garlic powder

The Night Before Serving

1. Arrange the ribs in the baking dish. Cut them into serving-sized portions, if you wish, or leave the slabs whole.
2. Combine the remaining ingredients in a medium bowl and pour over the ribs. Turn the ribs once to coat with marinade.
3. Cover with plastic wrap and refrigerate overnight.

About 6 Hours Before Serving

1. Remove the ribs from the refrigerator.
2. Start soaking 2 or 3 chunks of wood or a handful of wood chips, unless the smoker takes dry wood.
3. Fill the fire pan full of charcoal briquettes and start the fire.
4. When the coals turn grey, drain the wood pieces and add them to the coals. (For electric units: unless the smoker takes dry wood, drain the wood pieces and put them in their special pan.)
5. Set the water pan in place and fill almost full with hot water.
6. Put the cooking grill in place.
7. Arrange the ribs on the cooking grill or in a rib rack on the cooking grill.
8. Add the marinade to water pan or save to simmer for a sauce.
9. Cover. (Plug in electric smoker.) Smoke-cook about 5 to 5½ hours. After about 4 hours you may need to check the water pan and add a quart or so of hot water.

Makes about 4 servings

Arrange the ribs in a baking dish. Combine all the remaining ingredients for the marinade and pour them over the ribs. Turn to coat the ribs before covering and refrigerate overnight.

When the smoker is ready, place the ribs on a big rack or in a single layer on the grill. Add the remaining marinade to the water pan or save it to simmer as a sauce.

The combination of smoked pork and pineapple will win rave reviews.

Hong Kong Pork Chops

Make an Oriental meal from these chops by serving stir-fried snow peas, rice and tea. Mandarin orange slices and almond cookies for dessert complete the meal. Marinate the chops overnight or for just a few hours, whichever best suits your timetable.

8 to 10 (¾ inch thick) pork chops
⅓ cup soy sauce
¼ cup lemon juice
¼ cup molasses
¼ cup catsup
2 tablespoons sherry
1 clove garlic, minced

The Night Before Serving
1. Arrange the pork chops in the baking dish.
2. Combine all the remaining ingredients in a small bowl and pour over the chops.
3. Turn the chops so each gets coated with marinade.
4. Cover with plastic wrap and refrigerate overnight.

About 5½ Hours Before Serving
1. Remove the chops from the refrigerator.
2. Start soaking 2 or 3 chunks of wood or a handful of wood chips, unless the smoker takes dry wood.
3. Fill the fire pan full of charcoal briquettes and start the fire.
4. When the coals turn grey, drain the wood pieces and add them to the coals. (For electric units: unless the smoker takes dry wood, drain the wood pieces and put them in their special pan.)
5. Set the water pan in place and fill about ¾ full with hot water.
6. Put the cooking grill in place.
7. Arrange the chops on the cooking grill. Pour the marinade into the water pan.
8. Cover. (Plug in electric smoker.) Smoke-cook about 4½ to 5 hours. After about 4 hours you may need to check the water pan and add a quart or so of hot water.

Makes 6 to 8 servings

Make-Ahead Egg Rolls to go with Hong Kong Pork Chops

While you wait for Hong Kong Pork Chops to smoke-cook, appease your guests' appetites with these tasty egg roll appetizers. Many supermarkets, as well as oriental specialty shops, carry frozen egg roll dough. By making a big batch, you will have the appetizers on hand when you want them. If you own an electric wok, you can use it to deep-fry the egg rolls.

1 package (16 ounces) frozen egg roll dough, enough for 20 egg rolls
2 cans (16 ounces each) chop suey vegetables, drained and chopped
2 cans (6½ ounces) shrimp, well-drained
2 teaspoons soy sauce
½ teaspoon garlic powder
½ teaspoon onion salt
Oil for deep frying

1. Defrost the sheets of egg roll dough for about 10 minutes.
2. Combine the vegetables, shrimp, soy sauce, garlic powder and onion salt in a large mixing bowl. Mix thoroughly.
3. Put 2 tablespoons of the vegetable mixture in the center of each thawed sheet of dough.
4. Fold the side closest to you over the filling. Bring the right and then the left sides of the sheet over the filling. Dip your finger in water and run it over the edges of the dough. Fold the remaining side over and press gently to seal. The egg rolls can be frozen at this point.
5. To deep-fry: preheat the oil in the deep fryer as the manufacturer directs. Fry about 3 minutes or until golden brown and drain on paper towels.

Makes 20 Egg Rolls

Down South Barbecued Ribs

Molasses is the ingredient that makes these ribs so delicious! You can cut the "fire" of the marinade by reducing the amount of hot pepper sauce.

4 pounds spareribs
1/3 cup molasses
1/3 cup prepared mustard
1/4 cup soy sauce
1/4 cup vinegar
1 tablespoon Worcestershire sauce
1/2 to 1 teaspoon hot pepper sauce

The Night Before Serving
1. Put the ribs in a shallow baking dish or pan.
2. Combine all the remaining ingredients in a medium bowl and pour over the ribs.
3. Turn the ribs to coat completely with marinade.
4. Cover with plastic wrap and refrigerate overnight.

About 6 Hours Before Serving
1. Remove the ribs from the refrigerator.
2. Start soaking 2 or 3 chunks of wood or a handful of wood chips, unless the smoker takes dry wood.
3. Fill the fire pan full of charcoal briquettes and start the fire.
4. When the coals turn grey, drain the wood pieces and add them to the coals. (For electric units: unless the smoker takes dry wood, drain the wood pieces and put them in their special pan.)
5. Set the water pan in place and fill with hot water.
6. Put the cooking grill in place.
7. Lift the ribs from the marinade and arrange on the cooking grill or in a rib rack.
8. Cover. (Plug in electric smoker.) Smoke-cook about 5 to 5½ hours or until the meat begins to pull away from bone. After about 4 hours, check the water pan and add a quart or so of hot water, if necessary.

Makes 4 servings

Snappy Apple Relish to go with Down South Barbecued Ribs

Snappy Apple Relish, a tart, fresh-tasting condiment, is delicious with barbecued ribs. For a Southern-style picnic, you could also serve corn pudding, turnip greens, a big tossed salad, hot biscuits with strawberry jam, plus an array of relishes and a generous display of rich desserts.

4 medium-sized tart apples
2 tablespoons lemon juice
1/2 cup sugar
1/3 cup chopped dill pickle
1/4 cup cider vinegar
1/4 cup chopped onion

1. Core the apples and cut them into small strips about the size of matchsticks.
2. Sprinkle the cut strips with lemon juice to prevent browning.
3. Stir together all remaining ingredients in a medium-sized bowl.
4. Add the apples and toss to mix. Chill before serving.

Makes about 4 cups relish

Shanghai Spareribs

Sweet but spicy, these ribs soak up a piquant flavor from an unexpected ingredient — orange marmalade.

4 to 6 pounds spareribs
1 cup orange marmalade
½ cup water
½ cup soy sauce
1 clove garlic, minced
1 teaspoon ground ginger
Dash hot pepper sauce

The Night Before Serving
1. Place the ribs in a baking dish. Cut them into serving-sized portions, if you wish, or leave the slabs whole.
2. Combine all the remaining ingredients in a medium bowl and pour over the ribs. Turn the ribs once to coat with the marinade.
3. Cover with plastic wrap and refrigerate overnight.

About 6 Hours Before Serving
1. Remove the ribs from the refrigerator.
2. Start soaking 2 or 3 chunks of wood or a handful of wood chips, unless the smoker takes dry wood.
3. Fill the fire pan full of charcoal briquettes and start the fire.
4. When the coals turn grey, drain the wood pieces and add them to the coals. (For electric units: unless the smoker takes dry wood, drain the wood pieces and put them in their special pan.)
5. Put the water pan in place and fill almost full with hot water.
6. Set the cooking grill in place.
7. Arrange the ribs on the cooking grill or in a rib rack on the cooking grill.
8. Add the marinade to the water pan or save to baste ribs occasionally during cooking.
9. Cover. (Plug in electric smoker.) Smoke-cook about 5 to 5½ hours. After about 4 hours, check the water pan and add a quart or so of hot water, if necessary.

Makes 4 to 6 servings.

Stir-Fry Spinach to go with Shanghai Spareribs

Stir-Fry Spinach, an easy dish to prepare, would be delicious with Shanghai Spareribs, plain rice and perhaps a fruit compote with fresh lychee nuts added for a dinner with an oriental accent. Be careful not to overcook the vegetables, the spinach really should be just heated through and not too limp.

2 teaspoons lemon juice
1½ tablespoons soy sauce
1 teaspoon sugar
2 tablespoons cooking oil
1 medium onion, sliced
1 cup sliced fresh mushrooms
1½ cups diagonally sliced bok choy or celery
½ pound fresh spinach leaves, washed and stemmed

1. Combine the lemon juice, soy sauce and sugar in a cup and set it aside.
2. Heat the oil in a large skillet or wok and stir-fry the onion, mushrooms and bok choy for 2 minutes.
3. Add the spinach and lemon-soy mixture.
4. Stir-fry for about 2 minutes or until the onion and bok choy are tender-crisp and the spinach is barely limp.

Makes about 6 servings

PORK

Lemon–Thyme Country Ribs

Country-style ribs are very meaty, almost boneless cuts that are perfect for smoke-cooking. Instead of the lemon-thyme marinade, you could marinate the ribs in barbecue sauce or fruit juice, if you like.

4 pounds country-style ribs
3 lemons
2 tablespoons sugar
2 tablespoons oil
1 teaspoon salt
½ to 1 teaspoon thyme
⅛ teaspoon hot pepper sauce

About 6 Hours Before Serving

1. Arrange the ribs in the baking dish or in a heavy-duty plastic bag.
2. Grate the peel from 1 of the lemons and reserve. Juice all 3 lemons.
3. Combine the grated lemon peel, juice and all the remaining ingredients in a small bowl and pour over the ribs.
4. Cover with plastic wrap or close the bag securely and refrigerate for about 1 hour.
5. Start soaking 2 or 3 chunks of wood or a handful of wood chips, unless the smoker takes dry wood.
6. Fill the fire pan full of charcoal briquettes and start the fire.
7. Remove the ribs from the refrigerator.
8. When the coals turn grey, drain the wood pieces and add them to coals. (For electric units: unless the smoker takes dry wood, drain the wood pieces and put them in their special pan.)
9. Put the water pan in place and fill almost full with hot water.
10. Set the cooking grill in place.
11. Arrange the ribs on the cooking grill. Add the marinade to the water pan.
12. Cover. (Plug in electric smoker.) Smoke-cook about 4½ hours.

Makes about 6 servings

Ruby Crisp Dessert to go with Lemon–Thyme Country Ribs

Tart-sweet and scrumptious, this grapefruit dessert is a refreshing way to end a dinner featuring Lemon-Thyme Country Ribs. If you have room on the smoker's grill or if you have a double grill, you could cook Smoker Roasted Corn on the Cob or Herbed Smoked Tomatoes (see "Smoker Side Dishes") with the ribs.

"Filling"
6 large red grapefruit
3 tablespoons granulated sugar
2 tablespoons flour
½ teaspoon cinnamon
¼ teaspoon nutmeg

Topping
½ cup firmly-packed brown sugar
½ cup flour
½ cup regular oatmeal or quick-cooking (not instant)
¼ cup butter

1. Peel, section and seed the grapefruit (save any juice for other uses).
2. Arrange the grapefruit sections in a greased 8-inch square or round baking dish or pan.
3. Stir together the 3 tablespoons granulated sugar, 2 tablespoons flour and spices and sprinkle over the grapefruit.
4. Combine the brown sugar, flour and oatmeal; cut in the butter.
5. Sprinkle the sugar-oatmeal mixture over the grapefruit.
6. Bake in a preheated 375°F oven for 30 minutes or until top is browned.
7. Serve warm or cold.

Makes 6 servings

Ribs and Kraut

The perfect flavor team goes into the smoker and comes out absolutely delicious. You will be pleased with the savory results.

6 **pounds spareribs**
1½ **pounds sauerkraut**
¼ **cup finely chopped onion**
1 **cup tomato juice or sauce**
1 **tablespoon brown sugar**
1 **tablespoon caraway seed**

About 6 Hours Before Serving

1. Remove the ribs from the refrigerator.
2. Start soaking 2 or 3 chunks of wood or a handful of wood chips, unless the smoker takes dry wood.
3. Fill the fire pan full of charcoal briquettes and start the fire.
4. When the coals turn grey, drain the wood pieces and add them to the coals. (For electric units: unless the smoker takes dry wood, drain the wood pieces and put them in their special pan.)
5. In the water pan, combine the sauerkraut, onion and all the remaining ingredients.
6. Put the water pan in place and add just enough water to fill about ⅔ full.
7. Put the cooking grill in place.
8. Arrange the ribs on the cooking grill or in a rib rack on the cooking grill.
9. Cover. (Plug in electric smoker.) Smoke-cook about 5 to 5½ hours.
10. Check the water pan after about 3 hours, adding more water, if necessary, to keep the kraut very moist.
11. Serve the ribs with the kraut.

Makes 6 to 8 servings

Alpine Potatoes to go with Ribs and Kraut

These Swiss-style potatoes are first boiled then shredded and browned in a skillet to make an unusual potato dish with a crisp brown crust — perfect with Ribs and Kraut.

4 **medium potatoes**
4 **ounces Swiss cheese**
1 **medium onion, peeled**
5 **tablespoons butter, divided**
1 **teaspoon salt**
⅛ **teaspoon white pepper**
5 **or 6 parsley springs**

1. Cook the potatoes in boiling salted water until tender. Cool and peel.
2. Shred the potatoes and cheese and toss lightly to mix.
3. Chop the onion finely.
4. In a large skillet, melt 3 tablespoons butter.
5. Add the onion and cook until tender, about 5 minutes.
6. Stir the onion into the potatoes along with the salt and pepper.
7. Add the remaining 2 tablespoons butter to the skillet and melt.
8. Spread the potatoes in the skillet leaving just enough space around the edge of the skillet to check browning.
9. Cook, uncovered, over medium high heat about 5 minutes, or until bottom is browned and crisp.
10. Turn out onto a serving plate with the browned side up. Garnish with parsley.

Makes 4 to 6 servings

PORK

Ham with Currant–Orange Glaze

If you start with a full-cooked ham, you will be enjoying this tasty recipe in a few hours. You also can use the tangy glaze on a smoke-cooked fresh ham, brushing it on for the last few hours of cooking.

1 (6- to 8-pound) fully
    cooked ham
Whole cloves (optional)
1 jar (9 ounces) currant
    jelly
¼ cup orange juice
    concentrate, undiluted
1 teaspoon prepared
    horseradish
1 teaspoon dry mustard

About 3½ Hours Before Serving

1. Turn the ham fat side up and score the fat in diamonds. Garnish with whole cloves, if desired.
2. Start soaking 2 or 3 chunks of wood or a handful of wood chips, unless the smoker takes dry wood.
3. Fill the fire pan full of charcoal briquettes and start the fire.
4. Heat the jelly, orange juice concentrate, horseradish and mustard in a small saucepan until the jelly melts, stirring to blend.
5. When the coals turn grey, drain the wood pieces and add them to the coals. (For electric units: unless the smoker takes dry wood, drain the wood pieces and put them in their special pan.)
6. Put the water pan in place and fill with hot water.
7. Set the cooking grill in place.
8. Place the ham in the center of the cooking grill and brush generously with the jelly mixture.
9. Cover. (Plug in electric smoker.) Smoke-cook about 3 hours. Brush with any remaining glaze during the last half hour.

Makes about 12 servings

Blueberry Salad using Ham with Currant–Orange Glaze

Ham with Currant-Orange Glaze can make an encore in an unusual fresh fruit salad. Perfect for a fancy luncheon or light supper, this salad features a ginger-spiced yogurt dressing.

1 pint blueberries
Leaf lettuce, Romaine,
    curly endive or iceberg
    lettuce
2 to 3 cups cubed smoke-
    cooked ham
2 fresh peaches, nectarines
    or large plums, sliced
1 cup sliced celery
8 ounces plain
    unsweetened yogurt
2 tablespoons orange
    marmalade
½ teaspoon ground ginger

1. Wash the blueberries and drain them well.
2. Line a salad bowl with greens and arrange the ham, peaches, celery and blueberries in bowl.
3. Stir together the yogurt, marmalade and ginger and spoon over salad.

Makes 6 servings

Fruit-Stuffed Pork Roast

A perfect combination of flavors: rich and juicy pork, plus sweet-sour fruits and aromatic wood smoke. This recipe makes an extra-special treat for a family or company feast.

1 (3-pound) boneless pork loin roast, rolled and tied
1 cup dried apricots
½ cup orange juice
1 lemon, sliced
½ teaspoon salt

About 6 Hours Before Serving

1. Take the meat out of refrigerator and let it stand.
2. In a small saucepan, combine the apricots, orange juice, lemon and salt. Cover and simmer about 20 minutes or until the apricots are tender.
3. Uncover and simmer until very thick. Remove from the heat and let cool while preparing the fire.
4. Start soaking 2 or 3 chunks of wood or a handful of wood chips, unless the smoker takes dry wood.
5. Fill the fire pan full of charcoal briquettes and start the fire.
6. With a sharp knife, cut several deep slashes in the roast.
7. Stuff the slashes with the fruit mixture.
8. Spread any remaining fruit mixture over top of roast.
9. When the coals turn grey, drain the wood pieces and then add to the fire. (For electric units: put the wood pieces in their special pan.)
10. Put the water pan in place and fill with hot water.
11. Set the cooking grill in place.
12. Put the roast in the center of the cooking grill. Insert a meat thermometer into the center of largest muscle and away from a pocket of stuffing.
13. Cover. (Plug in electric smoker.) Smoke-cook 4 to 5 hours or until the meat thermometer reaches 170°F. After about 4 hours, check the water pan; add hot water, if necessary.

Makes about 8 servings

Claret Soup to go with Fruit-Stuffed Pork Roast

Complementing the Fruit-Stuffed Pork Roast, this piquant, cherry-berry "soup" can be served before the main dish or as a dessert. If fresh fruit is out of season and you cannot find unsweetened frozen fruit, use frozen cherries and berries (packaged with the least sugar possible) and reduce the brown sugar to ¼ cup. When the soup has cooled slightly, taste it; if it is too sweet, stir in ¼ cup lemon juice before adding the claret.

½ pound fresh or unsweetened frozen red tart cherries
½ pound fresh or unsweetened frozen blackberries
1 cup water
⅔ cup packed brown sugar
2 teaspoons cornstarch
¼ teaspoon salt
⅛ teaspoon cinnamon
⅛ teaspoon cardamom
1 cup claret
1 cup dairy sour cream

1. Wash, stem and pit cherries. Wash the berries. Thaw frozen fruit.
2. Put the fruit in a blender with the water and blend until smooth.
3. In a saucepan, stir together the brown sugar, cornstarch, salt, cinnamon, and cardamom.
4. Stir in the cherry mixture; cook and stir over medium heat until the mixture comes to a boil and is smooth and thickened.
5. Cool slightly, then stir in the claret.
6. Chill thoroughly.
7. Top each serving with dollop of sour cream.

Makes 6 to 8 servings

PORK

Hawaiian Ham Slices

Here is an excellent recipe to try the first time you use your smoker. It is very simple to fix and a fool-proof winner for a novice. Old hands at smoke-cooking will appreciate the ease of preparation, as well as the great flavor.

2 center-cut ham slices (about 1 pound each)
1 can (8 ounces) pineapple slices in pineapple juice
¼ cup brown sugar
1 teaspoon dry mustard
½ teaspoon pumpkin pie spice (optional)

About 3 Hours Before Serving

1. Remove the meat from the refrigerator. Drain the pineapple, reserving the juice. Set the slices aside.
2. In a small mixing bowl, combine the juice with all the remaining ingredients.
3. Start soaking 1 or 2 chunks of wood or a scant handful of wood chips, unless the smoker takes dry wood.
4. Fill the fire pan half full with charcoal briquettes and start the fire.
5. When the coals turn grey, drain the wood pieces, and add them to the coals. (For electric units: unless the smoker takes dry wood, drain the wood pieces and put them in their special pan.)
6. Set the water pan in place and fill half full with hot water.
7. Put the cooking grill in place.
8. Arrange the ham steaks on the cooking grill.
9. Brush the steaks with half the juice mixture. Top the steaks with the pineapple slices and brush with the remaining juice mixture.
10. Cover. (Plug in electric smoker.) Smoke-cook about 2½ hours or until meat is hot through.

Makes 4 to 6 servings

Kauai Cocktail Dessert to go with Hawaiian Ham Slices

A tart-flavored, sophisticated treat, you can make Kauai Cocktail Dessert with a frozen daiquiri mix or with limeade concentrate. Either way, it is a fitting finale for Hawaiian Ham Slices.

1 fresh pineapple or 2 cans (15¼ ounces each) pineapple slices in juice
1 cup light rum
1 can (6 ounces) frozen daiquiri mix or limeade concentrate, thawed
2 cups sugar
½ cup cornstarch
⅛ teaspoon salt

1. Cut the outer skin from the pineapple. Remove the core. Cut the fruit into chunks about 2 to 3 inches across.
2. Place half of the fruit and juice and ½ cup of the rum in a blender and chop coarsely. Repeat with the remaining fruit and rum. There should be about 3½ cups of chopped pineapple and juice.
3. Stir together the pineapple-rum mixture and daiquiri mix. Let stand at least 2 hours to develop the flavor.
4. Combine the sugar, cornstarch and salt in a saucepan. Add the pineapple-rum mixture. Cook and stir over medium heat until the mixture comes to a boil and is clear and thickened.
5. Chill thoroughly. To serve, spoon the "cocktail" into dessert glasses or use it as an ice cream topping.

Makes about 8 servings

Hawaiian Ham Slices feature a glaze of pineapple juice, brown sugar and spice.

PORK

Bavarian Pork Roast

Hearty and delicious, this roast and kraut combo is great for a company meal any time of the year. The sauerkraut simmers in pork juices in the water pan and develops a succulent flavor.

1 (6-pound) pork loin roast
2 pounds sauerkraut
2 apples, cored and
　　chopped
1 tablespoon caraway seed
½ teaspoon celery salt

About 8 Hours Before Serving
1. Insert a meat thermometer in the center of the largest muscle of the roast.
2. Combine the sauerkraut, apples and seasonings in the water pan.
3. Start soaking 2 or 3 chunks of wood or a handful of wood chips, unless the smoker takes dry wood.
4. Fill the fire pan full of charcoal briquettes and start the fire.
5. When the coals turn grey, drain the wood pieces and add them to the coals. (For electric units: unless the smoker takes dry wood, drain the pieces and add them to their special pan.)
6. Set the water pan in place and add enough hot water to fill almost full.
7. Put the cooking grill in place.
8. Place the meat in the center of the cooking grill.
9. Cover. (Plug in electric smoker.) Smoke-cook about 7½ hours or until the meat thermometer reaches 170°F. After about 4 hours you may need to check the water pan and add hot water.

Makes about 8 servings

Caraway Crisps to go with Bavarian Pork Roast

Bring out the Caraway Crisps while waiting for Bavarian Pork Roast to finish smoke-cooking. These delicious little nibbles are excellent with before-dinner drinks or on an appetizer tray with a dip and raw vegetables.

1 medium potato, cooked
　　and peeled
½ medium onion
¼ cup butter, softened
1 cup all-purpose flour
¼ cup grated Parmesan
　　cheese
½ teaspoon baking powder
½ teaspoon celery or garlic
　　salt
1 teaspoon caraway seed
　　Grated Parmesan cheese

1. Shred the potato and onion.
2. Mix the potato and onion with butter, then add the flour, cheese, baking powder, celery salt, and caraway seed. Mix until blended.
3. Pinch off pieces of the dough and form them into balls ½ inch in diameter.
4. Arrange the balls several inches apart on a greased baking sheet.
5. Press the balls flat with the bottom of a glass dipped in grated Parmesan cheese.
6. Bake the crisps in a preheated 375°F oven 20 to 25 minutes, or until browned and crisp.
7. Place them on a wire rack. Serve warm or cooled.

Makes about 3 dozen crisps

Savory Smoked Sausage Patties

If you have a double-decker grill, cook a vegetable such as new potatoes, sweet potatoes or acorn squash underneath the sausage patties. A vegetable also can be added to the water pan. Either way, the vegetable will be flavored with sausage drippings.

1½ pounds bulk pork sausage
Barbecue sauce, catsup or chili sauce (optional)

About 2½ Hours Before Serving

1. Form the sausage into 6 patties.
2. Start soaking 2 or 3 chunks of wood or a handful of wood chips, unless the smoker takes dry wood.
3. Fill the fire pan about ⅔ full with charcoal briquettes and start the fire.
4. When the coals turn grey, drain the wood pieces and add them to the coals. (For electric units: unless the smoker takes dry wood, drain the wood pieces and put them in their special pan.)
5. Put the water pan in place and fill about half full with hot water. (If you wish, add new potatoes, halved sweet potatoes or peeled and chunked acorn squash to the middle grill or to the water pan.)
6. Set the cooking grill in place.
7. Arrange the sausage patties on the cooking grill. Brush with barbecue sauce, catsup or chili sauce, if desired.
8. Cover. (Plug in electric smoker.) Smoke-cook about 2 hours.

Makes 4 to 6 servings

Squash Blossom Cups to go with Savory Smoked Sausage Patties

Each spicy cup makes a delectable container for your favorite fruits. You can pile the cups with sliced oranges, bananas, pineapple, grapes, then top with a dollop of sour cream or yogurt and sprinkle on some toasted nuts. Serve the fruit cups with Savory Smoked Sausage as a side dish or dessert for a delightful supper.

1 double piecrust recipe
1½ cups cooked hubbard or acorn squash, puréed
⅓ cup honey
½ teaspoon salt
1 teaspoon pumpkin pie spice
2 eggs, beaten
1 tablespoon lemon juice
1 cup milk

1. Prepare the piecrust recipe.
2. Roll out the dough and cut it into eight small circles to fit into a muffin tin or individual tart pans.
3. Line each muffin-holder with a circle of dough and crimp the edges.
4. For the filling, mix all the remaining ingredients thoroughly and pour into the unbaked tart crusts. Bake at 450°F for 15 minutes, lower the oven to 325°F and bake another 20 minutes. When cool, top with fresh fruits to serve.

Makes 8 servings

CHICKEN

There's a smoked chicken for every kind of Sunday — or any day — in this chapter. Marinate chicken in Italian dressing for a bird to delight the whole gang at a casual outdoor get-together. Marinate chicken in herbs and wine and — *voilá* — you have a superb entrée for an intimate, candle-lit supper. Chicken Scheherezade suggests a Near Eastern banquet and Chicken South of the Border calls for a Mexican fiesta.

Easy Italian Chicken

No marinade could be simpler — all you need is bottled salad dressing, or Italian dressing made from a packaged mix. The longer you marinate the chicken, the spunkier the flavor. Try this easy salad dressing marinade for beef, pork and fish, too.

1 (6-pound) roasting chicken or capon
1 cup bottled or prepared Italian salad dressing

The Night Before Serving
1. Put the chicken in a large baking dish.
2. Pour half the salad dressing into the cavity of the chicken; brush the remainder over the chicken.
3. Cover the chicken with plastic wrap.
4. Refrigerate overnight.

About 7½ Hours Before Serving
1. Remove the chicken from the refrigerator.
2. Start soaking 2 or 3 chunks of wood or a handful of wood chips, unless the smoker takes dry wood.
3. Fill the fire pan full of charcoal briquettes and start the fire.
4. When the coals turn grey, drain the wood pieces and add them to the coals. (For electric units: unless the smoker takes dry wood, drain the wood pieces and put them in their special pan.)
5. Set the water pan in place and fill almost full with hot water.
6. Put the cooking grill in place.
7. Place the chicken in the center of the cooking grill. Add the marinade to the water pan.
8. Cover. (Plug in electric smoker.) Smoke-cook about 6 or 7 hours or until a leg moves easily in its joint. After about 4 hours you may need to check the water pan and add a quart or so of hot water.

Makes 6 to 8 servings

Put the chicken in a large baking pan and pour half the dressing into the cavity of the chicken. Brush the remaining dressing over the chicken before covering and refrigerating overnight.

Place the marinated chicken in the center of the grill when the smoker is ready. Allow 6 or 7 hours of smoke-cooking. The chicken is done when a leg moves easily in its joint.

Serve Easy Italian Chicken with Asparagus in Foil for an easy Italian feast.

Roast Chicken Rosemary

Rosemary is a classic flavoring for chicken. You will get extra fragrance and flavor by tossing a small handful of dried rosemary onto the coals when you add the wood. It's a delightful touch — try it!

1 (7-pound) roasting chicken
1 teaspoon seasoned salt
1 teaspoon salt
1 tablespoon rosemary, crushed

About 8 Hours Before Serving

1. Rub the chicken inside and out with the salts and rosemary.
2. Let the chicken stand at room temperature while preparing the fire.
3. Start soaking 2 or 3 chunks of wood or a handful of wood chips, unless the smoker takes dry wood.
4. Fill the fire pan full of charcoal briquettes and start the fire.
5. When the coals turn grey, drain the wood and add them to coals. (For electric units: unless the smoker takes dry wood, drain the wood pieces and put them in their special pan.)
6. Set the water pan in place and fill with hot water.
7. Put the cooking grill in place.
8. Place the chicken in the center of the cooking grill.
9. Cover. (Plug in electric smoker.) Smoke-cook about 6 to 7 hours or until a leg moves easily in its joint. After 4 hours you may need to check the water pan and add a quart or so of hot water.

Makes 6 to 8 servings

Spinach Bake to go with Roast Chicken Rosemary

For a Sunday chicken dinner with a difference, serve this custardy spinach dish with Roast Chicken Rosemary, plus a salad of tomato slices and artichoke hearts, some French or sourdough rolls and perhaps peach shortcake or fresh fruit for dessert.

1 pound fresh spinach
1 cup plain unsweetened yogurt or 1 cup dairy sour cream or 1 package (8 ounces) cream cheese cubed
3 eggs
1 small onion
½ teaspoon summer savory or basil
½ teaspoon salt
⅛ teaspoon white pepper

1. Wash the spinach thoroughly and remove any tough stems.
2. Cook the spinach in only the water that clings to the leaves for about 4 minutes in a covered saucepan. The spinach should be just barely limp.
3. In a blender, combine the spinach with the remaining ingredients and blend until smooth.
4. Pour the mixture into a buttered 1-quart baking dish or souffle dish.
5. Bake in a preheated 325°F oven about 35 minutes or until a knife inserted near the center comes out clean.

Makes 6 servings

Herb and Wine Chicken

Use your favorite herb to flavor these tasty birds, or experiment with an herb that is new to you. When whole fryers are on special at the market, stock up on them to smoke-cook. You can buy a bargain and fix a feast!

2 whole fryers (about 2½ pounds each)
⅔ cup white wine
2 tablespoons oil or melted butter
1½ teaspoons rosemary, crushed (or basil, tarragon, oregano, savory or chervil)
½ teaspoon salt
⅛ teaspoon hot pepper sauce

The Night Before Serving
1. Put the chickens in a large heavy-duty plastic bag.
2. Combine all the remaining ingredients in a small bowl and pour into the bag.
3. Close the bag securely and tip to coat the chickens completely with marinade.
4. Refrigerate overnight or at least several hours.

About 5 Hours Before Serving
1. Remove the chicken from the refrigerator.
2. Start soaking 2 or 3 chunks of wood or a handful of chips, unless the smoker takes dry wood.
3. Fill the fire pan full of charcoal briquettes and start the fire.
4. When the coals turn grey, drain the wood pieces and add them to the coals. (For electric units: unless the smoker takes dry wood, drain the wood pieces and add them to their special pan.)
5. Set the water pan in place and fill almost full with hot water.
6. Put the cooking grill in place.
7. Lift the chickens from the bag to the cooking grill.
8. Pour the marinade over the chickens and into the water pan.
9. Cover. (Plug in electric smoker.) Smoke-cook about 4 to 4½ hours or until a chicken leg twists easily in its socket.

Note: If you wish, you can throw a few tablespoons of dried herbs along with the wood pieces to add extra aroma.

Makes 6 to 8 servings

Filbert-Cheese Dessert to go with Herb and Wine Chicken

Garnish this elegant molded dessert with melon slices and serve additional cubes of melon with lime juice along with it to make a tart-sweet contrast to Herb and Wine Chicken. If you have room on the smoker's grill, or if you have a double grill, Fruited Rice and Smoker Mushrooms (see "Smoker Side Dishes") would go excellently with smoked chicken. Add a mixed vegetable salad dressed with herb and wine vinegar and some pita bread for a delicious banquet.

Filbert–Cheese Dessert to go with Herb and Wine Chicken   (continued)

1½ **cups cottage cheese**
1 **envelope unflavored gelatin**
¼ **cup water**
1 **cup milk, divided**
1 **can (6 ounces) frozen limeade concentrate, thawed**
½ **cup whipping cream**
2 **tablespoons sugar**
¼ **teaspoon vanilla**
¾ **cup chopped toasted filberts**

1. Put the cottage cheese in a blender and blend until smooth.
2. In a small saucepan, sprinkle the gelatin over the water to soften.
3. Add ½ cup of the milk and heat over low heat until the gelatin dissolves.
4. Stir in the remaining milk along with the limeade and cottage cheese.
5. Whip the cream until light and fluffy.
6. Add the sugar and vanilla to the whipped cream and mix briefly.
7. Fold the whipped cream into the cheese mixture.
8. Fold in the filberts.
9. Turn the dessert into a 5-cup mold.
10. Chill until firm.

Makes 6 to 8 servings

Herb and Wine Chicken, shown with Filbert - Cheese Dessert, makes a sophisticated meal.

CHICKEN

Chicken South of the Border

Mildly flavored with a whiff of spices, this chicken recipe could team up with an avocado salad, some refried beans, tortilla chips and fresh fruit for a marvelous meal.

2 frying chickens, cut up
1½ cups tomato juice
¼ cup oil
¼ cup chopped onion
2 tablespoons lemon juice
2 tablespoons Worcestershire sauce
1 teaspoon salt
1 teaspoon cumin
½ teaspoon garlic powder
¼ teaspoon lemon pepper
¼ teaspoon hot pepper sauce

The Night Before Serving

1. Arrange the chicken in a baking dish or heavy-duty plastic bag.
2. Combine all the remaining ingredients in a small bowl and pour over the chicken.
3. Cover with plastic wrap or close the bag securely.
4. Refrigerate overnight. Turn the chicken in the marinade occasionally, if you think of it.

About 4½ Hours Before Serving

1. Remove the chicken from the refrigerator.
2. Start soaking 2 or 3 chunks of wood or a handful of wood chips, unless the smoker takes dry wood.
3. Fill the fire pan full of charcoal briquettes and start the fire.
4. When the coals turn grey, drain the wood pieces and add them to the coals. (For electric units: unless the smoker takes dry wood, drain the wood pieces and put them in their special pan.)
5. Put the water pan in place and fill almost full with hot water.
6. Set the cooking grill in place.
7. Arrange the chicken pieces on the cooking grill.
8. Pour the marinade into the water pan.
9. Cover. (Plug in electric smoker.) Smoke-cook about 3½ to 4 hours.

Makes 6 to 8 servings

Avocado Picante Salad to go with Chicken South of the Border

Make the spunky dressing several hours in advance to blend the flavors, then drizzle it over the avocado and orange slices for a south-of-the-border salad. Grapefruit can replace the orange slices, if you choose.

Dressing

½ cup salad oil
⅓ cup white wine vinegar
1 can (4 ounces) whole green chilies, drained
1 teaspoon dry mustard
½ teaspoon chili powder
1½ teaspoons salt
1 teaspoon basil
1 clove garlic

Salad

6 large Romaine leaves
3 large seedless oranges
2 large avocados
1 medium red onion

1. Combine all the dressing ingredients in a blender.
2. Blend until the chilies are very finely chopped.
3. Let the dressing stand several hours to blend the flavors.
4. Place the Romaine leaves on 6 individual salad plates.
5. Peel and section the oranges, removing as much of the white membrane as possible.
6. Arrange the orange sections in pinwheel patterns on the Romaine leaves.
7. Peel, seed and slice the avocados in thin wedges.
8. Arrange the wedges in between the orange sections.
9. Slice the onion in thin rings.
10. Place the rings on top of the avocado and oranges.
11. Pour the dressing over the salad to serve.

Makes 6 servings

Chicken Scheherezade

Yogurt is a favorite chicken marinade in the Near East. The yogurt coating, mildly flavored with curry, takes on additional color and richness when the chicken is smoked.

1 **frying chicken, cut up**
1 **cup plain yogurt**
¼ **cup finely chopped green onion**
1 **teaspoon curry powder**
1 **teaspoon salt**

About 4 Hours Before Serving
1. Remove the chicken from the refrigerator.
2. Combine the yogurt with all the remaining ingredients in a small mixing bowl.
3. Arrange the chicken in a shallow pan or baking dish or in a heavy-duty plastic bag.
4. Pour the yogurt mixture over the chicken, turning the chicken to coat all sides.
5. Cover loosely and let it stand while preparing the smoker.
6. Start soaking 2 or 3 chunks of wood or a handful of wood chips, unless the smoker takes dry wood.
7. Fill the fire pan full of charcoal briquettes and start the fire.
8. When the coals turn grey, drain the wood pieces and add them to the coals. (For electric units: unless the smoker takes dry wood, drain the wood pieces and put them in their special pan.)
9. Set the water pan in place and fill with hot water.
10. Put the cooking grill in place.
11. Arrange the chicken pieces on the cooking grill.
12. Cover. (Plug in electric smoker.) Smoke-cook about 3 to 4 hours.

Makes 4 servings

Spicy Eggplant Dip to go with Chicken Scheherezade

Cut up strips of pita bread and toast them to scoop up this exotic eggplant dish. Ranking somewhere between a condiment and a vegetable side dish, Spicy Eggplant Dip might also be served as an appetizer. The eggplant shells are used as serving bowls.

1 **large eggplant**
1 **large onion**
2 **medium tomatoes**
1 **green pepper**
½ **pound fresh mushrooms**
2 **cloves garlic**
½ **cup olive oil**
2 **cups tomato sauce**
2 **tablespoons lemon juice**
1 **teaspoon sugar**
1 **teaspoon basil**
1 **teaspoon cumin**
½ **teaspoon cinnamon**
½ **teaspoon chili powder**
¼ **cup chopped cilantro or parsley**
2 **teaspoons salt**

1. Cut a thin slice lengthwise off the side of the eggplant to form an eggplant "boat."
2. Scoop out the meat, leaving a ¼-inch thick shell. Cover the shell and chill it.
3. Chop or slice the eggplant, onion, tomatoes, green pepper, mushrooms, and garlic.
4. Heat the oil in a large skillet or saucepan. Add the vegetables and cook and stir over medium-high heat for 3 to 4 minutes.
5. Stir in the tomato sauce, lemon juice, sugar, basil, cumin, cinnamon, chili powder, cilantro, and salt. Simmer uncovered about 30 minutes or until thick.
6. Chill the vegetable mixture. To serve, spoon the mixture into the eggplant shell.

Makes about 6 servings

Lemon-Buttered Chicken

Lemon-Buttered Chicken develops a beautiful rich brown color and a unique flavor in the smoker. The lemon flavor does not predominate, but you will be intrigued by the very special taste.

1 **frying chicken, cut up**
2 **lemons**
2 **tablespoons butter,**
  melted
1 **teaspoon salt**
½ **to 1 teaspoon dry mustard**
¼ **teaspoon lemon pepper**

About 4 Hours Before Serving
1. Remove the chicken from the refrigerator.
2. Grate the peel from the lemons, then squeeze the juice from the lemons.
3. Combine the lemon peel, juice, butter and seasonings.
4. Brush or rub the lemon-butter mixture over all surfaces of the chicken. Cover loosely and let stand while preparing smoker.
5. Start soaking 2 or 3 chunks of wood or a handful of wood chips, unless the smoker takes dry wood.
6. Fill the fire pan full of charcoal briquettes and start the fire.
7. When the coals turn grey, drain the wood pieces and add them to the coals. (For electric units: unless the smoker takes dry wood, drain the wood pieces and add them to their special pan.)
8. Set the water pan in place and fill with hot water.
9. Put the cooking grill in place.
10. Arrange the chicken pieces on the cooking grill.
11. Cover. (Plug in electric smoker.) Smoke-cook about 3 to 4 hours.

Makes 4 servings

Herb-Glazed Butternut Rings *to go with Lemon-Buttered Chicken*

A decorative way to serve winter squash, Herb-Glazed Butternut Rings have a delightful glaze of honey, pecans and rosemary. You could cook Asparagus in Foil (see "Smoker Side Dishes") along with the chicken and, if you have room on the grill, heat some garlic bread wrapped in foil for the last hour of cooking time.

1 **or 2 small butternut or**
  acorn squash
½ **teaspoon salt**
¼ **cup butter**
¼ **cup chopped pecans**
3 **tablespoons honey**
½ **teaspoon crushed**
  rosemary

1. Slice the squash crosswise into ½-inch thick rings.
2. Remove the seeds, strings and peel.
3. In a large saucepan, heat 1 inch of water to boiling and add the salt and squash rings.
4. Cover and cook 15 to 20 minutes or until tender.
5. Melt the butter in a large skillet.
6. Add the pecans and cook and stir over medium-high heat until lightly browned.
7. Stir in the honey and rosemary. Mix until blended.
8. Add the squash rings.
9. Heat, stirring and turning the squash to coat with the glaze.

Makes 4 to 6 servings

Smoked Chicken Livers

We suggest you serve smoked livers as elegant appetizers. Their flavor is just too rich to serve as a main course.

1 pound chicken livers
¼ cup oil, melted butter or bacon drippings

About 1½ Hours Before Serving

1. Start soaking 1 or 2 chunks of wood or a small handful of wood chips, unless your smoker takes dry wood.
2. Fill the fire pan ⅔ full of charcoal briquettes and start the fire.
3. When the coals turn grey, drain the wood pieces and add them to the coals. (Electric smokers: unless the smoker takes dry wood, drain the pieces and put them in their special pan.)
4. Put the water pan in place and fill with hot water.
5. Oil the cooking grill and set it in place.
6. Drain the livers well and brush each liver with oil.
7. Arrange the livers on the well-oiled cooking grill.
8. Cover. (Plug in electric smoker.) Smoke-cook about 1½ hours or until the livers are done.

Makes about 6 appetizer servings

Double–Dip Appetizer Platter to go with Smoked Chicken Livers

Along with Smoked Chicken Livers, offer your guests a double choice of dips — one for dipping fruit slices and one for raw vegetables and assorted crackers.

Fruit Curry Dip

1½ cups cottage cheese
½ cup dairy sour cream
1 teaspoon curry
½ teaspoon garlic salt
1 (8-ounce) can juice-packed crushed pineapple, well drained
½ cup chopped unpeeled red apple

1. Using the highest speed of your mixer or blender, beat together the cottage cheese, sour cream, curry and garlic salt until they are smooth.
2. Stir in the pineapple and apple.
3. Cover and chill before serving.

Makes about 2½ cups of dip

Blue Cheese Dip

1½ cups cottage cheese
½ cup sour cream
1 cup (4 ounces) crumbled blue cheese
2 tablespoons chopped green onion
¼ teaspoon garlic salt
1 teaspoon Worcestershire sauce
1 tablespoon lemon juice
½ cup plain unsweetened yogurt.

1. Mix together the cottage cheese, sour cream and blue cheese using the highest speed of your mixer or blender.
2. Beat in the onion, garlic salt, Worcestershire sauce and lemon juice.
3. Fold in the yogurt.
4. Cover and chill before serving.

Makes about 2½ cups of dip

Honey–Lime Chicken

Fresh lime juice and honey give the chicken a delicate piquant flavor. The sweet-sour marinade is good on pork steaks, too.

2 fryers (about 2 to 2½ pounds each), cut up
2 teaspoons grated lime peel
⅓ cup lime juice
¼ cup honey
1 teaspoon celery seed
1 teaspoon salt

The Night Before Serving
1. Put the chicken pieces in a large heavy-duty plastic bag.
2. In small bowl or measuring cup, combine all the remaining ingredients and blend.
3. Pour the marinade over the chicken, turning the pieces to coat them completely.
4. Close the bag securely.
5. Refrigerate overnight or at least several hours, turning occasionally.

About 5 Hours Before Serving
1. Remove the chicken from the refrigerator.
2. Start soaking 2 or 3 chunks of wood or a handful of chips, unless the smoker takes dry wood.
3. Fill the fire pan full of charcoal briquettes and start the fire.
4. When the coals turn grey, drain the wood pieces and add them to the coals. (For electric units: unless the smoker takes dry wood, drain the wood pieces and add them to their special pan.)
5. Set the water pan in place and fill with hot water.
6. Put the cooking grill in place.
7. Lift chickens from marinade to the cooking grill.
8. Pour the marinade over the chickens and into the water pan.
9. Cover. (Plug in electric smoker.) Smoke-cook about 4 to 4½ hours.

Makes about 6 servings

Banana–Honey Dressing to go with Honey–Lime Chicken

Tangy Banana-Honey Dressing and smoked chicken are a marvelous combination. You could use the dressing as a topping for open-faced sandwiches of sliced Honey-Lime Chicken, or as a dressing for a fruit platter or tossed salad to serve with the smoked chicken.

2 ripe bananas
½ cup salad oil
¼ cup honey
2 tablespoons herb vinegar
1 teaspoon grated lime peel
4 tablespoons lime juice
½ teaspoon salt
½ teaspoon paprika
1 teaspoon celery seed

1. Peel and mash the bananas.
2. Beat in all the remaining ingredients or mix in a blender.
3. Chill before serving over an open-faced sandwich or salad.

Makes about 1¼ cups dressing

TURKEY, DUCK AND GOOSE

Turkey looks and tastes magnificent when smoke-cooked. Served hot or cold, a handsomely bronzed turkey will be the center of attention. Equally spectacular are smoke-cooked, golden-colored duck and goose. The duck's crispy skin glazed with a piquant sauce satisfies the most demanding epicurean. Turkey legs, turkey pieces and turkey rolls can be smoke-cooked with extravagantly rich-tasting results, too.

Smoked Turkey

A gourmet's fantasy come true — here is a delicacy you can have anytime you want! Smoke-cooked turkeys are absolutely beautiful. They take on a rich, mahogany color and subtle smoke flavor. Once you have smoke-cooked a turkey you will never put one in your oven again. Even though it may take a little longer to cook in cold weather, turkeys can be smoke-cooked for Thanksgiving and Christmas.

1 **(12-pound) turkey,**
    completely thawed
1 **teaspoon salt**
¼ **teaspoon pepper**
½ **cup celery leaves**
2 **small onions, quartered**

About 12 to 13 Hours Before Serving
1. Remove the turkey from refrigerator.
2. Sprinkle it inside and out with salt and pepper.
3. Stuff the celery leaves and quartered onions inside the turkey. Insert a meat thermometer in the thigh, with the tip away from the bone.
4. Start soaking 2 or 3 chunks of wood or a handful of wood chips, unless the smoker takes dry wood.
5. Fill the fire pan heaping full of briquettes and start the fire.
6. When the coals turn grey, drain the wood pieces and add them to the coals. (For electric units: unless the smoker takes dry wood, drain the wood pieces and put them in their special pan.)
7. Put the water pan in place and fill almost full with water.
8. Put the cooking grill in place.
9. Put the turkey in the center of the cooking grill.
10. Cover. (Plug in electric smoker.) Smoke-cook about 12 hours or until a leg moves easily in its joint or the meat thermometer reaches 180°F. Check the water pan every 4 hours during cooking time and add hot water, if necessary. On some units you may need to add charcoal after 6 or 7 hours of cooking. See "Crisis Cooking" for how to add charcoal. Remember that cooking will take much longer if bird is not completely thawed, if it is less than 65°F outside or windy.

Makes about 10 to 12 servings

DUCK AND GOOSE

Smoked Turkey is delicious without being marinated. Just salt and pepper the inside and stuff the bird with celery leaves and onions.

Place a meat thermometer in the thigh with the tip away from the bone. When the smoker is ready, set the turkey in the center of the grill.

About 12 hours later, Smoked Turkey will be deliciously bronzed and ready to astonish your friends and family.

The traditional turkey, cooked in an untraditional manner, is a glorious sight on a holiday table.

TURKEY

Turkey Teriyaki

Leave the turkey whole, or cut into parts before marinating. It will take you about 3 hours less cooking time if you cut up the turkey. Also, the teriyaki flavor will be a little stronger on the cut parts.

1 (about 10-pound) turkey, thawed
¾ cup soy sauce
½ cup sherry
¼ cup oil
1 tablespoon ginger
1 tablespoon dry mustard
1 teaspoon garlic powder

The Night Before Serving

1. Arrange the whole turkey or turkey pieces in a baking dish or heavy-duty plastic bag.
2. Combine all the remaining ingredients in a small bowl until blended.
3. Pour the marinade into and over the turkey. Turn the turkey so the marinade coats it completely.
4. Cover with plastic wrap or close the bag securely.
5. Refrigerate overnight, turning the turkey in the marinade occasionally.

About 9 to 10 Hours Before Serving

1. Remove the turkey from the refrigerator.
2. Start soaking 2 or 3 chunks of wood or a handful of wood chips, unless the smoker takes dry wood.
3. Fill the fire pan full of charcoal briquettes and start the fire.
4. When coals turn grey, drain the wood pieces and add them to the coals. (For electric units: unless the smoker takes dry wood, drain the wood pieces and add them to their special pan.)
5. Put the water pan in place and fill almost full with hot water.
6. Put the cooking grill in place.
7. Lift the turkey from the marinade and place it on the cooking grill. If you want, insert a meat thermometer in the thickest part of the thigh, away from the bone. If you have cut up the turkey try to leave some space between the pieces. Pour the marinade over the turkey into the water pan.
8. Cover. (Plug in electric smoker.) Smoke-cook a whole turkey about 10 hours or until the meat thermometer reaches 180°F. Smoke-cook turkey pieces 6 to 7 hours. Check the water pan every 4 hours and add a quart or so of hot water, if necessary. On some units you may need to add charcoal after 6 to 7 hours of cooking. See "Crisis Cooking" for how to add charcoal.

Makes 10 to 12 servings

Ginger–Grapefruit Ice for Turkey Teriyaki

Echoing the ginger-spicy accents of Turkey Teriyaki, this cooling dish is a delectable conclusion to a smoked turkey feast or can be served with the turkey as a side dish. Plain rice, some pickled Japanese-style relishes (available in oriental specialty shops) and stir-fried oriental vegetables would be good accompaniments to Turkey Teriyaki.

Ginger–Grapefruit Ice for Turkey Teriyaki **(continued)**

2 medium grapefruit
2 cups sugar
4 cups water
¼ teaspoon salt
3 or 4 drops yellow food coloring
2 tablespoons chopped crystalized ginger
⅛ teaspoon ground ginger (optional)

1. Grate the peel from the grapefruit and squeeze the juice from them. Set the juice and peel aside.
2. Boil the sugar and water together for 5 minutes.
3. Cool the sugar-water, then stir in the grapefruit juice and peel.
4. Add the salt, food coloring, and ginger. Mix thoroughly.
5. Turn the mixture into ice cube trays or shallow metal pans and freeze until almost firm.
6. Whirl the ice in a blender or beat until smooth, then return it to the freezer until solid.

Makes 8 to 10 servings

Caveman Turkey Legs

A big platter of smoked turkey legs looks like a primitive feast. Of course, smoking is one of the most ancient ways of preserving meat. Smoke-cooking the modern way using this simplified marinade shows that some progress has been made since our cave-dwelling ancestors.

4 to 6 turkey legs
1 envelope onion soup mix
1 cup oil
1 cup red wine vinegar
½ cup soy sauce
½ teaspoon garlic powder

The Night Before Serving
1. Place the turkey legs in a heavy-duty plastic bag.
2. Combine all the remaining ingredients and pour them over the turkey.
3. Close the bag securely and refrigerate overnight, turning the legs occasionally.

About 6 to 7 Hours Before Serving
1. Remove the turkey from the refrigerator.
2. Start soaking 2 or 3 chunks of wood or a handful of wood chips.
3. Fill the fire pan full of charcoal briquettes and start the fire.
4. When the coals turn grey, drain the wood pieces, and add them to the coals. (For electric units, plug in. Drain the wood pieces and put them in their special pan.)
5. Put the water pan in place and fill almost full with water.
6. Put the cooking grill in place.
7. Arrange the turkey legs on the cooking grill.
8. Pour the excess marinade into the water pan.
9. Cover and smoke-cook about 6 to 6½ hours. After about 4 hours you may need to check the water pan in a charcoal smoker and add a quart or so of hot water.

Makes 6 to 8 servings

Barbecued Turkey Rolls

A couple of smoked turkey rolls are easy to smoke-cook to serve a crowd. Cut the recipe in half, if you are just cooking for the family. Water Pan Potatoes and Silver Turbaned Apples (see "Smoker Side Dishes") would be good with the turkey.

- 2/3 cup chili sauce
- 1/3 cup red wine
- 3 tablespoons molasses
- 2 tablespoons instant minced onion
- 1 teaspoon Worcestershire sauce
- 1 tablespoon grated orange peel
- 1/2 cup water
- 1 teaspoon salt
- 1 teaspoon dry mustard
- 1/2 teaspoon cayenne sauce
- 2 (2-pound) frozen turkey rolls, thawed

About 4 or 5 hours before serving.

1. Combine all the ingredients, except the turkey rolls. Set aside while preparing the smoker.
2. Start soaking 2 or 3 chunks of wood or a handful of wood chips.
3. Fill the fire pan full of charcoal briquettes and start the fire.
4. When the coals turn grey, drain the wood pieces and add them to the coals. (For electric units, plug in. Drain the wood pieces and put them in their special pan.)
5. Put the water pan in place and fill almost full with water.
6. Put the cooking grill in place.
7. Place the turkey rolls on the cooking grill.
8. Brush generously with the chili sauce mixture. Insert a meat thermometer in one of the rolls.
9. Cover and smoke-cook about 4 to 5 hours or until the thermometer registers 180°F. After about 4 hours you may need to check the water pan in a charcoal smoker and add water.

Makes 8 to 10 servings

Watermelon Punch to go with Barbecued Turkey Rolls

Food and beverages that are fun to look at and fun to eat delight youngsters — and kids at heart. Watermelon punch, served in a carved watermelon rind, and Barbecued Turkey Rolls would be perfect for a family picnic.

- 1 large watermelon
- 1 quart pineapple juice, chilled
- 1 quart ginger ale or lemon-lime carbonated beverage, chilled
- 1 can (6 ounces) frozen lemonade or limeade concentrate, thawed

1. Pick a melon that is evenly-shaped and wide in diameter. Cut a thin slice from the bottom so the melon won't roll. Tie a piece of string around the melon above the halfway point and trace lightly with a pencil. For a fancy edge, cut scallops around the melon with a short sharp knife. Use a longer knife to slide in the cuts at several places around the melon to loosen the fruit in the middle.
2. Lift off the top. Scoop out all the fruit from top and bottom and cut some into balls.
3. Press scraps of fruit through a sieve or food mill, removing the seeds, and reserve the juice. You should have 6 to 8 cups of juice.
4. Put the balls in the melon shell. Cover shell with plastic wrap and chill thoroughly.
5. In a large container combine the watermelon juice and all the remaining ingredients.
6. Pour the punch into the watermelon shell to serve. Keep any remaining punch chilled until needed to refill shell.

Makes 3 to 4 quarts of punch.

Tarragon Turkey Pieces

By cutting a small turkey into pieces before marinating and smoking you get extra flavor, and shorten the cooking time. Do try turkey other than at holidays — you will find it a bargain and a flavor treat.

1 (5- to 7-pound) turkey, cut up
1 cup tarragon vinegar
½ cup oil
1 tablespoon instant minced onion
1 teaspoon salt
1 teaspoon tarragon leaves, crushed
1 teaspoon lemon pepper

The Night Before Serving

1. Arrange the turkey pieces in a baking dish or heavy-duty plastic bag.
2. Combine all the remaining ingredients and pour them over the turkey.
3. Cover with plastic wrap or close the bag securely.
4. Refrigerate overnight. Turn the turkey pieces in the marinade occasionally, if you think of it.

About 6 to 7 Hours Before Serving

1. Remove the turkey from the refrigerator.
2. Start soaking 2 or 3 chunks of wood or a handful of wood chips, unless the smoker takes dry wood.
3. Fill the fire pan full of charcoal briquettes and start the fire.
4. When the coals turn grey, drain the wood pieces and add them to the coals. (For electric units: unless the smoker takes dry wood, drain the wood pieces and put them in their special pan.)
5. Put the water pan in place and fill almost full with hot water.
6. Put the cooking grill in place.
7. Arrange the turkey pieces on the cooking grill.
8. Pour the marinade into the water pan.
9. Cover. (Plug in electric smoker.) Smoke-cook about 6 to 6½ hours. After about 4 hours you may need to check the water pan and add a quart or so of hot water.

Makes 6 to 8 servings

Cold Cucumber Soup to go with Tarragon Turkey Pieces

Sipped from chilled mugs or served more formally in soup bowls, Cold Cucumber Soup revives dwindling spirits on hot summer days. By the time your guests finish the zesty soup they will be ready to appreciate the rich flavor of Tarragon Turkey Pieces.

4 medium cucumbers, peeled
2 limes
3 cups plain unsweetened yogurt
2 green onions
1½ teaspoons salt
¾ teaspoon dried dill weed

1. Shred the cucumbers. Set them aside to drain.
2. Grate the limes and squeeze the juice from them. Set the peel and juice aside in separate bowls.
3. In a blender, combine the yogurt, onion, salt, dill weed, lime juice and half of the reserved lime peel. Blend until smooth.
4. Add the reserved cucumbers. Blend until pureed.
5. Chill the soup. At serving time, garnish with the remaining lime peel.

Makes 6 to 8 servings

Easy Oriental Duckling

There is no flavor that compares with this crispy, deep-brown duckling. Cook several ducklings for a crowd and impress them!

1 (5-pound) duckling
1 cup bottled teriyaki sauce
2 tablespoons molasses or
   dark corn syrup
½ to 1 teaspoon dry mustard
½ to 1 teaspoon garlic
   powder

The Night Before Serving

1. Put the duckling in a glass bowl or heavy-duty plastic bag.
2. Combine all the remaining ingredients in a small bowl and pour over the duckling, being sure the marinade goes all over the inside as well as the outside of the bird.
3. Cover the bowl with plastic wrap or close the bag securely.
4. Refrigerate overnight or at least several hours, turning the duckling in the marinade occasionally.

About 7 Hours Before Serving

1. Remove the duckling from the refrigerator.
2. Start soaking 2 or 3 chunks of wood or a handful of wood chips, unless the smoker takes dry wood.
3. Fill the fire pan full of charcoal briquettes and start the fire.
4. When the coals turn grey, drain the wood pieces and add them to the coals. (For electric units: unless the smoker takes dry wood, drain the wood pieces and put them in their special pan.)
5. Put the water pan in place and fill almost full with hot water.
6. Set the cooking grill in place.
7. Lift the duckling from the bag to the center of the cooking grill. Prick the surface of the duckling in many places with a two-tined fork, so the fat can drain off.
8. Pour the marinade over the duckling and into the water pan.
9. Cover. (Plug in electric smoker.) Smoke-cook about 6 hours or until a duck leg twists easily in its socket. After about 4 hours you may need to check the water pan and add a quart or so of hot water.

Makes 3 to 4 servings

Oriental Salad to go with Easy Oriental Duckling

Crisp-cooked vegetables, smartly dressed in a Japanese-style dressing make a crunchy salad to serve with Easy Oriental Duckling. For a variation, you could add a cup of bean sprouts or canned oriental vegetables, or substitute iceberg lettuce for part of the spinach leaves. Plain rice and a dessert of fresh pineapple and papaya drizzled with lime juice would harmonize with the duck and Oriental Salad. Or, you might want to surprise your guests by producing the dessert from the smoker. Turn to the chapter called "Smoker Side Dishes" for a luscious treat called Rummy Pineapple.

Oriental Salad to go with Easy Oriental Duckling **(continued)**

Salad

- **1 cup diagonally sliced green beans**
- **1 medium onion, sliced thin**
- **½ cup thin sliced carrots**
- **1 cup shredded chinese celery cabbage (nappa)**

Dressing

- **2 tablespoons toasted sesame seeds**
- **⅔ cup sake or sherry**
- **2 tablespoons soy sauce**
- **¼ cup salad oil**
- **2 teaspoons grated lemon peel**
- **3 tablespoons lemon juice**

1. Steam the green beans, onion and carrots until they are tender, but still crisp.
2. Chill the steamed vegetables, then mix them with the remaining salad ingredients.
3. Combine all of the dressing ingredients and pour the dressing over the salad.

Makes 4 to 6 servings

Easy Oriental Duckling, with its crispy, brown skin, is irresistible.

Sweet and Hot Duckling

Duckling coated inside and out with a spicy marinade is exquisite. A simple stir-fried, vegetable dish and plain rice are all the accompaniments this exotically flavored duckling needs.

1 (5-pound) duckling
1 cup orange marmalade
½ cup soy sauce
¼ cup sherry
1 clove garlic, minced
1 teaspoon dry mustard
½ teaspoon cayenne sauce

The Night Before Serving
1. Put the duckling in a glass bowl or heavy-duty plastic bag.
2. Combine all the remaining ingredients in a small bowl and pour over the duckling, being sure the marinade goes all over the inside as well as the outside of the bird.
3. Cover the bowl with plastic wrap or close the bag securely.
4. Refrigerate overnight or at least several hours, turning the duckling in the marinade occasionally.

About 7 Hours Before Serving
1. Remove the duckling from the refrigerator.
2. Start soaking 2 or 3 chunks of wood or a handful of wood chips, unless the smoker takes dry wood.
3. Fill the fire pan full of charcoal briquettes and start the fire.
4. When the coals turn grey, drain the wood pieces and add them to the coals. (For electric units: unless the smoker takes dry wood, drain the wood pieces and put them in the special pan.)
5. Put the water pan in place and fill almost full with hot water.
6. Set the cooking grill in place.
7. Lift the duckling from the bag to the center of the cooking grill. Prick the surface of the duckling in many places with a two-tined fork, so the fat can drain off.
8. Pour the marinade over the duckling.
9. Cover. (Plug in electric smoker.) Smoke-cook about 6 hours or until a duck leg twists easily in its socket. After about 4 hours you may need to add water to the water pan.

Makes 3 to 4 servings

Broccoli Stir-Fry to go with Sweet and Hot Duckling

To accompany Sweet and Hot Duckling, offer Broccoli stir-fry and plain rice. When your guests ask what exotic vegetable is mixed with the broccoli, they will be surprised to learn it is just the broccoli stem cleverly cut into thin circles.

1 bunch (1 pound) broccoli
1 medium onion
½ sweet red pepper
2 tablespoons oil
1 tablespoon lemon juice
1 tablespoon soy sauce

1. Wash the broccoli and cut off the flowerets. Set them aside.
2. Cut the broccoli stem in thin slices parallel to the base of the stalk to make irregular circle shapes.
3. Slice the onion in thin slices.
4. Cut the pepper in small cubes.
5. Heat the oil in a wok or large skillet and stir-fry the broccoli stems and onion for about 2 minutes.
6. Add the broccoli flowerets and stir-fry for 2 more minutes or until the vegetables are tender-crisp.
7. Add the red pepper and stir briefly to heat.
8. Sprinkle the lemon juice and soy sauce over the vegetables.

Makes 6 servings

Plum-Delicious Duckling

An easy plum glaze flavors this duckling. If you have room on the grill, cook Asparagus in Foil or Silver Plated Carrots (see "Smoker Side Dishes") to accompany the succulent duckling.

1 (5-pound) duckling
½ cup plum jam
1 tablespoon lemon juice
1 tablespoon soy sauce

About 7 Hours Before Serving
1. Remove the duckling from the refrigerator.
2. Start soaking 2 or 3 chunks of wood or a handful of wood chips, unless the smoker takes dry wood.
3. Fill the fire pan full of charcoal briquettes and start the fire.
4. When the coals turn grey, drain the wood pieces and add them to the coals. (For electric units: unless the smoker takes dry wood, drain the wood pieces and put them in special pan.)
5. Put the water pan in place and fill almost full with hot water.
6. Set the cooking grill in place.
7. Place the duckling in the center of the grill and prick the skin with a two-tined fork, so the fat can drain off.
8. Cover. (Plug in electric smoker.) Smoke-cook about 5 hours. After about 4 hours, check the water pan and add more water if necessary.
9. Mix the plum jam, lemon juice and soy sauce. Carefully lift the lid of the smoker and quickly brush the plum mixture on the duck.
10. Continue smoke-cooking for 1 more hour, or until a leg twists easily in its socket.

Makes 3 to 4 servings

Stuffed Plums to go with Plum-Delicious Duckling

Stuffed Plums are attractive, tasty morsels to serve with Plum-Delicious Duckling. Any variety of plum will do, as long as it is fresh and ripe.

4 to 6 plums
1 tablespoon plum brandy
¾ cup part-skim ricotta cheese
½ cup plain unsweetened yogurt
1 tablespoon chopped crystalized ginger
8 to 12 pecan halves

1. Slice the plums in half.
2. Whip the brandy, ricotta and yogurt until fluffy.
3. Stir in the ginger.
4. Mound a tablespoon of the ricotta mixture on top of each plum half.
5. Garnish each stuffed plum with a pecan.

Makes 3 to 4 servings

TURKEY

DUCK AND GOOSE

Smoked Goose

Frozen geese usually are available year-round and you often can buy fresh ones during the holiday season. You can smoke-cook one you have bagged yourself, of course. Stuff the goose, if you wish, using your favorite stuffing, or prepare as below.

1 goose (about 8 to 10 pounds) fresh or thawed, cleaned
½ teaspoon salt
½ teaspoon pepper
1 apple, cored and chopped
1 onion, quartered
1 stalk celery, chopped

About 10 Hours Before Serving

1. Remove the goose from the refrigerator. Sprinkle the cavity generously with salt and pepper, then stuff with apple, onion and celery.
2. Let the goose stand at room temperature while preparing the fire.
3. Start soaking 2 or 3 chunks of wood or a handful of wood chips, unless the smoker takes dry wood.
4. Fill the fire pan full of charcoal briquettes and start the fire.
5. When the coals turn grey, drain the wood pieces and add them to the coals. (For electric units: unless the smoker takes dry wood, drain the wood pieces and put them in their special tray.)
6. Set the water pan in place and fill with hot water.
7. Put the cooking grill in place.
8. Prick the surface of the goose in many places with a two-tined fork, so the fat can drain off.
9. Put the goose in the center of the cooking grill.
10. Cover. (Plug in electric smoker.) Smoke-cook about 8 to 10 hours or until a leg twists easily in its socket. After about 4 hours you may need to check the water pan and add a quart or so of hot water. You may have to replenish the charcoal in some units after about 7 hours. See ''Crisis Cooking'' for instructions.

Makes 8 to 10 servings

Cranberry Castle Cake to go with Smoked Goose

Baked in a fancy mold, Cranberry Castle Cake looks and tastes like an old-fashioned steamed pudding, but is much less trouble to make. Smoked Goose and Cranberry Castle Cake could become a holiday tradition at your house.

3 cups cranberries
3½ cups all-purpose flour
1 cup chopped pecans or walnuts
1 tablespoon baking soda
2 teaspoons baking powder
2 teaspoons cinnamon
½ teaspoon salt
2 teaspoons nutmeg
1 cup light molasses
2 tablespoons oil
¼ cup hot water
2 eggs
Whipped cream or hard sauce

1. Stir together the cranberries, flour, nuts, soda, baking powder and spices.
2. Blend the molasses, oil, hot water and eggs.
3. Add them to the dry ingredients and mix until blended.
4. Heavily grease and flour a fancy 1½-quart mold and pour in the batter.
5. Cover the top tightly with greased foil.
6. Bake in a preheated 350°F oven for 1½ hours or until a cake tester comes out clean. Remove the foil and bake another 15 minutes.
7. Turn the cake out of the mold and serve warm with whipped cream or hard sauce.

Makes 10 to 12 servings

GAME

The woodsy scent of juniper berries mingles with aromatic smoke when you smoke-cook quail, dove, pheasant or squab according to the Smoked Small Game Birds recipe. Those pleasant aromas wafting through the neighborhood may draw quite an audience for you to entertain with your favorite hunting sagas. If rabbit or squirrel is part of your catch, you could add a tablespoon or two of dried rosemary, basil or other herb to the coals, along with the wood, for intriguing flavor.

Sweet-Sour Cornish Hens

These little hens take on a lovely glaze and delightful flavor from bottled sweet-sour sauce. You could treat small game birds in the same way.

4 Rock Cornish game hens (about 1 pound each)
2 teaspoons salt
1 teaspoon lemon pepper
1 lemon, sliced
1 cup bottled sweet-sour sauce

About 5 Hours Before Serving
1. Sprinkle the hens inside and out with the salt and lemon pepper.
2. Stuff a lemon slice or two inside each hen.
3. Brush the birds liberally with sweet-sour sauce.
4. Start soaking 2 or 3 handfuls of wood or a scant handful of chips, unless the smoker takes dry wood.
5. Fill the fire pan full of charcoal briquettes and start the fire.
6. When the coals turn grey, drain the wood pieces and add them to the coals. (For electric units: unless the smoker takes dry wood, drain the wood pieces and put them in their special pan.)
7. Insert the water pan and fill it almost full with hot water.
8. Put the cooking grill in place.
9. Arrange the hens on the cooking grill and again brush generously with the sauce.
10. Cover. (Plug in electric smoker.) Smoke-cook about 4 hours or until richly brown and a leg moves easily in its joint.
11. Brush with any remaining sauce before serving.

Makes 4 to 6 servings

Lemon pepper and lemon slices give bottled sweet-sour sauce more bite. Sprinkle the hens inside and out with salt and lemon pepper.

Stuff a couple of lemon slices inside each hen.

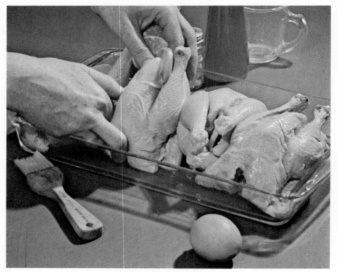

Brush the birds generously with sweet-sour sauce. Save some sauce to brush on the hens when they are on the grill.

Arrange the birds on the grill when the smoker is ready. Leave some space between them. Brush the hens with additional sweet-sour sauce.

Sweet-Sour Cornish Hens turn a handsome golden color when they are done.

Smoked Small Game Birds

Squab, quail, dove, duck or pheasant can all be cooked according to these directions. The results are delicious! Whether you give the birds a pre-soak in brine or not is up to you. Older, gamier birds would benefit from a little pretreatment. The size of the bird determines the number of servings. Quail and doves serve one apiece, ducks and pheasants can serve 2 or more.

1 quart water
¼ cup salt
3 to 4 small game birds, cleaned and plucked
12 juniper berries (or small onions, quartered and several sprigs of parsley)
¾ cup butter or bacon drippings (or 3 to 4 halved slices of bacon)

About 8 Hours Before Serving

1. Combine the water and salt and stir until the salt dissolves.
2. Put the birds in a heavy-duty plastic bag or deep glass bowl and pour the brine over them.
3. Put a plate on top of the bowl and weight it to hold the birds under the brine, or close bag securely.
4. Refrigerate an hour or two.
5. Drain the birds and rinse with cold water, then let them stand, uncovered, at room temperature while starting the fire.
6. Start soaking 2 or 3 chunks of wood or a handful of wood chips, unless the smoker takes dry wood.
7. Fill the fire pan full of charcoal briquettes and start the fire.
8. Put a few juniper berries or a piece of onion and some parsley in the cavity of each bird.
9. When the coals turn grey, drain the wood pieces and add them to the coals. (For electric units: unless the smoker takes dry wood, drain the wood pieces and put them in their special pan.)
10. Insert the water pan and fill it with hot water.
11. Set the cooking grill in place.
12. Brush the birds generously with butter or drippings, or arrange halved bacon slices across the breast of each bird.
13. Arrange the birds on the cooking grill.
14. Cover. (Plug in electric smoker.) Smoke-cook about 3 to 5 hours, depending on size of bird, or until a leg twists easily in its socket.

Makes 3 to 4 servings

Cauliflower Sour to go with Smoked Small Game Birds

A combination salad and vegetable dish, Cauliflower Sour is served cold and makes a good contrast to Smoked Small Game Birds. If you have room on the grill, smoke-cook Herbed Smoked Tomatoes (see "Smoker Side Dishes") with the birds.

1 large cauliflower
½ cup salad oil
½ cup lemon juice
2 tablespoons cider vinegar
½ teaspoon salt
¼ teaspoon tarragon
6 pimiento-stuffed green olives, sliced

1. Break the cauliflower into flowerets and steam until tender-crisp.
2. Mix together all the remaining ingredients except the olives and pour them over the cauliflower while the cauliflower is still hot.
3. Chill the cauliflower thoroughly.
4. Garnish with olive slices to serve.

Makes 4 to 6 servings

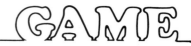

Smoke-Cooked Venison

Several days spent in a marinade helps reduce the gamy flavor of venison and adds a unique taste. Use the saddle (or loin) of venison or the haunch. Count on ¾ pound per serving and an hour per pound for cooking.

1 **venison saddle or haunch (5 pounds or more)**
1½ **cups red wine**
½ **cup red wine vinegar**
½ **cup oil**
½ **cup chopped onion**
1 **teaspoon oregano**
1 **clove garlic, minced**

Several Days Before Serving

1. Put the venison in a large bowl, enamel pan or heavy-duty plastic bag.
2. Combine all the remaining ingredients in a medium bowl and pour over the meat.
3. Refrigerate several days, turning occasionally.

About 6 Hours Before Serving

1. Remove the venison from the refrigerator.
2. Start soaking 2 or 3 chunks of wood or a handful or two of wood chips, unless the smoker takes dry wood.
3. Fill the fire pan full with charcoal briquettes and start the fire.
4. When the coals turn grey, drain the wood pieces and add them to coals. (For electric units: unless the smoker takes dry wood, drain the wood pieces and put them in their special pan.)
5. Set the water pan in place and fill almost full with hot water.
6. Put the cooking grill in place.
7. Lift the venison from the marinade and place in the center of the cooking grill.
8. Pour the remaining marinade into the water pan.
9. Cover. (Plug in electric smoker.) Smoke-cook about 5 hours for a 5 pound piece of venison. After about 4 hours, check the water pan and add a quart or so of hot water, if needed.

3/4 pound equals 1 serving

Swiss Rice to go with Smoke-Cooked Venison

Excellent with Smoked Venison, this rice dish is cooked in beef broth and has Swiss cheese stirred into it before serving. To go along with the delightful rice dish and Smoked Venison, select a vegetable salad and perhaps a stewed fruit compote.

2 **tablespoons butter**
1 **cup rice**
2¼ **cups beef broth**
½ **teaspoon salt**
¾ **cup grated Swiss cheese**

1. Melt the butter in a skillet and sauté the rice until light brown.
2. In a saucepan, bring the broth and salt to a boil and add the rice.
3. Cover and simmer for 15 to 20 minutes, until the rice is tender.
4. Stir in the grated cheese, mixing lightly with a fork until the cheese is stringy.

Makes 4 to 6 servings

Smoked Rabbit or Squirrel

For other variations, check the chicken recipes and try any of those marinades with either rabbit or squirrel.

**1 rabbit or squirrel,
    cleaned, dressed and
    cut up**
¼ cup butter or oil, melted
1 teaspoon salt
½ teaspoon pepper

About 5 Hours Before Serving
1. Brush the squirrel or rabbit with melted butter or oil. Sprinkle with salt and pepper.
2. Start soaking 2 or 3 chunks of wood or a handful of chips, unless the smoker takes dry wood.
3. Fill the fire pan full with charcoal briquettes and start the fire.
4. When the coals turn grey, drain the wood pieces and add them to the coals. (For electric units: unless the smoker takes dry wood, drain the wood pieces and put them in their special pan.)
5. Set the water pan in place and fill with hot water.
6. Put the cooking grill in place.
7. Arrange the rabbit or squirrel pieces on the cooking grill.
8. Cover. (Plug in electric smoker.) Smoke-cook about 4 hours.

Note: if you wish, add a tablespoon or two of dried rosemary, basil, tarragon or oregano to the coals along with the wood.

Makes 3 to 4 servings

Apple–Nut Muffins to go with Smoked Rabbit or Squirrel

Apple makes these tasty muffins extra moist. Served with a corn pudding and some sliced fresh tomatoes, Smoked Rabbit or Squirrel and these muffins will make a memorable meal. The recipe may be doubled.

**1 cup enriched all-purpose
    flour**
1½ tablespoons sugar
2 teaspoons baking powder
½ teaspoon salt
¼ teaspoon cinnamon
1 small egg, beaten
½ cup milk
1 tablespoon oil
**½ cup chopped peeled
    apple**
**¼ cup chopped pecans or
    walnuts**

1. Stir together the flour, sugar, baking powder, salt and cinnamon.
2. Combine the egg, milk and oil and add them to the dry ingredients all at once with apple and pecans.
3. Stir only until the flour is moistened.
4. Spoon into a greased or lined muffin pan.
5. Bake in a preheated 425°F oven 20 to 25 minutes.
Makes 6 muffins

SEAFOOD

Whether you fish the lakes, the streams, the high seas or just the local supermarket, the gentle, moist heat of smoke-cooking will bring out the best flavor of your fish. Some recipes call for soaking the fish in herb-seasoned brine, other recipes call for simple seasonings like lemon and pepper. Besides fish steaks, pan fish, fillets and whole large fish — smoked Lobster Tails, Smoked King Crab Legs and succulent Smoke-Cooked Shrimp can be part of your smoke-cooking repertoire.

Smoked Rainbow Trout

If the boss (or anyone else you want to impress) is coming for dinner, here is an impressive dish to serve! Whether you catch the trout yourself, buy it fresh or frozen, it makes an elegant entrée. Should you have any left over, refrigerate and serve the next day as a show-off appetizer! Each trout equals one serving. If you have more guests, just add more trout.

6 rainbow trout, cleaned
   (about 12 ounces each)
2 cups cold water
2 tablespoons salt
½ cup oil
1 lemon, sliced
6 bacon strips

About 3 Hours Before Serving

1. Arrange the trout in baking dish or heavy-duty plastic bag.
2. In a small mixing bowl or quart glass measure, combine the water and salt and stir until the salt dissolves to make a brine.
3. Pour the brine over the trout.
4. Cover the dish with plastic wrap or close the bag securely.
5. Refrigerate ½ hour.
6. Start soaking 2 or 3 chunks of wood or a handful of wood chips, unless the smoker takes dry wood.
7. Fill the fire pan almost full of charcoal briquettes and start the fire.
8. When the coals turn grey, drain the wood pieces and add them to the coals. (For electric units: unless the smoker takes dry wood, drain the wood pieces and put them in their special pan.)
9. Put the water pan in place and fill about ⅔ full with hot water.
10. Set the cooking grill in place.
11. Lift the trout from the brine and rinse with cold water.
12. Brush both sides of the trout with oil.
13. Insert lemon slices in each fish.
14. Cover each fish with a strip of bacon.
15. Arrange the fish on the cooking grill. Add the brine to water pan, if you wish, or discard it.
16. Cover. (Plug in electric smoker.) Smoke-cook about 2 to 3 hours, or until the fish is firm to the touch and flakes easily when tested with a fork.

Makes 6 servings (one trout each)

Smoked Rainbow Trout is simply flavored with lemon slices. Soak the trout in a salt brine for half an hour.

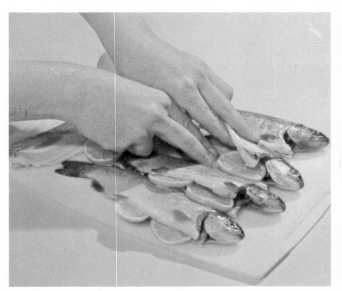

Take the trout from the brine and rinse them with cold water, brush with oil and insert lemon slices in each fish.

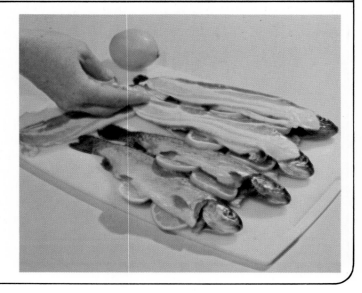

Cover each trout with a strip of bacon.

When the smoker is ready, place the trout with their bacon-blankets on the grill.

For an entrée or appetizer, Smoked Rainbow Trout is as elegant as it is delicious.

Smoky Snapper Fillets

Use small frozen fillets or bigger fillets from the fish market or fresh fish section of your supermarket. Slice a lime or lemon to heat in some butter, then brush or spoon the butter over the fillets just before serving — sensational!

2 to 3 pounds red snapper fillets
3 cups water
3 tablespoons salt
3 tablespoons seasoned salt
1 teaspoon celery seed
1 teaspoon mustard seed

About 4 Hours Before Serving

1. Arrange the fish fillets in a shallow baking dish or heavy-duty plastic bag.
2. Combine the water, salts and seasonings; stir until the salts dissolve to make a brine.
3. Pour the brine over the fish.
4. Cover the dish or close the bag securely.
5. Refrigerate at least ½ hour.
6. Start soaking 2 or 3 chunks of wood or a handful of wood chips, unless the smoker takes dry wood.
7. Fill the fire pan almost full with charcoal briquettes and start the fire.
8. When coals turn grey, drain the wood pieces and add them to the coals. (For electric units: unless the smoker takes dry wood, drain the wood pieces and put them in their special pan.)
9. Put the water pan in place and fill ¾ full with hot water.
10. Set the cooking grill in place.
11. Lift the fish fillets from the brine and rinse with clear water.
12. Arrange on the cooking grill. Add the brine to the water pan, if you wish, or discard it.
13. Cover. (Plug in electric smoker.) Smoke-cook about 2 to 3 hours or until the fish is firm to the touch and flakes easily when tested with a fork.

Makes about 6 servings

Arrange the fillets in a shallow baking dish. Combine the water, salts, celery seed and mustard seed to make a brine.

Pour the seasoned brine over the fillets. Cover and refrigerate at least half an hour.

Lift the fillets from the brine.

Rinse them in clear water.

Place the fillets on the grill and smoke-cook 2 to 3 hours or until the fish is firm and flakes easily when tested with a fork.

Smoky Snapper Fillets, garnished with lemon and parsley, are ready for a picnic or formal dinner.

Tomato Barbecued Halibut Steaks

Fix this feast for your most special guests. You can prepare other large fish steaks this same way. For hearty eaters, allow 1 steak per person. Those guests with small appetites can split a steak.

3 or 4 halibut steaks
1 can (8 ounces) tomato sauce with onions
3 tablespoons lemon juice
1 tablespoon instant minced onion
1 tablespoon sugar
1 tablespoon Worcestershire sauce
1 teaspoon salt
1 clove garlic, minced

About 4 Hours Before Serving

1. Place the halibut in a baking dish.
2. Combine all the remaining ingredients in a medium bowl and pour over the halibut.
3. Turn the steaks so both sides are coated with marinade.
4. Cover with plastic wrap and refrigerate 30 to 60 minutes.
5. Start soaking 2 or 3 chunks of wood or a handful of wood chips, unless the smoker takes dry wood.
6. Fill the fire pan about ¾ full with charcoal briquettes and start the fire.
7. When the coals turn grey, drain the wood pieces and add them to the coals. (For electric units: unless the smoker takes dry wood, drain the wood pieces and put them in their special pan.)
8. Set the water pan in place and fill almost full with hot water.
9. Put the cooking grill in place.
10. Arrange the halibut steaks on the cooking grill. Pour the marinade into the water pan.
11. Cover. (Plug in electric smoker.) Smoke-cook about 3 hours or until the fish flakes easily with a fork.

Makes 3 or 4 servings

Tomato Barbecued Halibut Steaks calls for making a tangy marinade that doubles as a barbecue sauce.

Combine all the sauce ingredients and pour them over the fish in a shallow baking dish. Cover with plastic wrap and refrigerate 30 to 60 minutes.

Place the halibut steaks on the grill with as much of the marinade on top as possible.

Pour any excess marinade through the grill into the water pan for additional flavor during smoke-cooking.

The barbecue marinade turns the halibut steaks an appetizing color.

SEAFOOD

Fisherman's Catch

Here is the way to cook pan fish such as bluegill, crappie and sunfish. The number of servings depends, of course, on the size of the fish. Fresh or thawed fish can be used.

6 small whole pan fish,
  fresh or thawed,
  cleaned
1 teaspoon salt
½ teaspoon pepper
¼ cup oil
3 bacon slices, halved

About 3 Hours Before Serving

1. Start soaking 2 or 3 chunks of wood or a handful of wood chips, unless the smoker takes dry wood.
2. Fill the fire pan about ¾ full with charcoal briquettes and start the fire.
3. Sprinkle the cavities of the fish with salt and pepper. Brush the outsides of the fish with oil.
4. When the coals turn grey, drain the wood pieces and add them to the coals. (For electric units: unless the smoker takes dry wood, drain the wood pieces and put them in their special pan.)
5. Set the water pan in place and fill about ⅔ full with hot water.
6. Put the cooking grill in place.
7. Arrange the fish on the cooking grill.
8. Top each fish with a half slice of bacon.
9. Cover. (Plug in electric smoker.) Smoke-cook about 2 to 2½ hours (depending on the size of the fish) or until the fish flakes when tested with a fork.

Makes about 4 to 6 servings

Orangerie Rice to go with Fisherman's Catch

Delightful with smoked fish, Orangerie Rice has crunchy water chestnuts in it and is garnished with cashews. Serve smoked pan fish and Orangerie Rice with broccoli and, perhaps, homemade ice cream for dessert.

¼ cup butter
½ cup chopped water
  chestnuts
2 tablespoons minced
  onion
1 tablespoon minced
  parsley
1 tablespoon grated orange
  peel
1 cup orange juice
1¼ cups water
1 teaspoon salt
1 cup regular rice
¼ cup cashews

1. Melt the butter in a skillet and add the water chestnuts and onion. Cook 5 minutes or until just tender.
2. Stir in all remaining ingredients except the rice and cashews. Heat to boiling.
3. Add the rice, cover and simmer 20 minutes, or until the rice is done. Garnish with cashews.

Makes about 4 to 6 servings

Smoked Fish Steaks

If you caught a big one, here is the way to cook it! Salmon, swordfish, halibut, turbot, almost any fish that can be cut into steaks is delicious when smoke-cooked. The flavor is rich and the texture of the cooked fish superb. After tasting smoke-cooked fish you will understand why fishermen like to take their smoke cookers along on fishing jaunts.

4 to 6 fish steaks (or one per serving)
2 cups cold water
3 tablespoons salt
1 tablespoon seasoned salt
¼ cup oil

About 3 Hours Before Serving

1. Place the fish steaks in a baking dish or heavy-duty plastic bag.
2. Combine the water, salt and seasoned salt in small mixing bowl or quart glass measure. Stir until the salt dissolves to make a brine.
3. Pour the brine over the fish.
4. Cover with plastic wrap or close the bag securely.
5. Refrigerate at least ½ hour.
6. Meanwhile start soaking 2 or 3 chunks of wood or a handful of wood chips, unless the smoker takes dry wood.
7. Fill the fire pan almost full with charcoal briquettes and start the fire.
8. When the coals turn grey, drain the wood pieces and put them on the coals. (For electric units: unless the smoker takes dry wood, drain the wood pieces and put them in their special pan.)
9. Put the water pan in place and fill about ⅔ full with hot water.
10. Set the cooking grill in place.
11. Lift the fish steaks from the brine and rinse under cold running water.
12. Brush the steaks with oil on both sides.
13. Arrange the fish on the cooking grill. Add the brine to the water pan, if you wish, or discard.
14. Cover. (Plug in electric smoker.) Smoke-cook about 2 to 3 hours or until the fish is firm to the touch and flakes easily when tested with a fork.

Makes 4 to 6 servings

Samoan Sauce to go with Smoked Fish Steaks

A cooling, crunchy topping, Samoan Sauce is a natural for Smoked Fish Steaks. If you do not want it on the fish, serve it as a dressing for fruit salad.

1 lemon
1½ cups plain unsweetened yogurt
¾ cup salted peanuts
½ cup flaked coconut
1 teaspoon curry powder

1. Grate the peel from the lemon.
2. Remove the white membrane and quarter and seed the lemon. Place it in a blender, along with the yogurt.
3. Blend until the lemon is puréed.
4. Add the peanuts, coconut and curry powder. Blend just until the peanuts are coarsely chopped.
5. Refrigerate until ready to serve.

Makes about 2½ cups of sauce

Smoked Lobster Tails

Smoking takes longer than broiling or boiling, the other methods for cooking lobster tail, but the results are well worth the wait! Your can "steam" lobster tails (or whole lobsters) in the smoke-cooker without adding wood chips. Select the size of the lobster tails to match your guests' appetite; 6 to 8 ounces per tail will make a generous portion.

**Lobster tails, thawed
    (1 tail per serving)
Butter**

About 2 Hours Before Serving
1. Start soaking 2 or 3 chunks of wood or a handful of wood chips, unless the smoker takes dry wood.
2. Fill the fire pan about ¾ full of charcoal briquettes and start the fire.
3. When the coals turn grey, drain the wood and add them to the coals. (For electric units: unless the smoker takes dry wood, drain the wood pieces and add them to their special pan.)
4. Put the water pan in place and fill about ⅔ full with hot water.
5. Arrange the lobster tails on the cooking grill.
6. Cover. (Plug in electric smoker.) Smoke-cook about 1 to 1½ hours or until flesh is white and firm.

Note: If you wish, you can butterfly the lobster tails before cooking. Using poultry shears or heavy kitchen scissors, cut through middle of the shell and down the entire length of the tail. Press open along the cut with your thumbs and then fold tail open. Brush with melted butter before arranging the tails on the cooking grill.

1 lobster tail equals 1 serving

Montego Bay Melon to go with Smoked Lobster Tails

Cantaloupe and honeydew balls steep in rum and watermelon juice making a spectacular center-piece to accompany Smoked Lobster Tail. You could substitute a fruit-flavored liqueur for the rum, if you prefer.

**1 cantaloupe
1 honeydew melon
¼ small watermelon
½ cup sugar
2 to 4 tablespoons dark rum**

1. Cut the cantaloupe and honeydew in half and scoop out the seeds.
2. Cut the melon into balls with a melon ball cutter or measuring teaspoon.
3. Put the balls in a large serving dish.
4. Cut the watermelon in cubes and press them through a food mill or sieve. You'll need 2 cups watermelon juice.
5. Mix the sugar and rum until the sugar dissolves, then stir into the watermelon juice.
6. Pour the juice-rum mixture over the melon balls.
7. Cover and chill several hours or overnight.

Makes about 8 servings

Smoked Whole Fish

Here is how to cook the big ones. Whether you catch it in the sea, a lake or the market, nothing is better than a salmon, lake trout, red snapper or any other big fish cooked in the smoker. Count on about 3 servings from every 2 pounds of fish. If your fish is too big to fit in the smoker, cut off its head and tail. You can stuff a big fish before putting it in the smoker; use stuffing prepared from a mix or your favorite recipe.

1 **large whole fish (about 5
   to 10 pounds), cleaned**
1 **teaspoon seasoned salt**
¼ **teaspoon pepper**
1 **lemon, sliced**
½ **cup oil**

About 4½ to 5 Hours Before Serving

1. Sprinkle the cavity of the fish with salt and pepper and line with the lemon slices.
2. Start soaking 2 or 3 chunks of wood or a handful of wood chips, unless the smoker takes dry wood.
3. Fill the fire pan full of charcoal briquettes and start the fire.
4. When the coals turn grey, drain the wood pieces and add them to the coals. (For electric units: unless the smoker takes dry wood, drain the wood pieces and put them in their special pan.)
5. Put the water pan in place and fill about ¾ full with hot water.
6. Set the cooking grill in place.
7. Brush outside of fish with oil, then arrange on cooking grill.
8. Cover. (Plug in electric smoker.) Smoke-cook about 4 to 4½ hours or until fish flakes when tested with a fork.

Makes 3 servings per every 2 pounds fish

Fruit Relish to go with Smoked Whole Fish

Perfect with smoked fish, this spicy relish features fresh blueberries. You can make a dessert out of it by serving it with cream cheese on crackers, or serve it with the fish.

1 **stick cinnamon**
8 **whole cloves**
½ **teaspoon nutmeg**
½ **cup honey**
¼ **cup lemon juice**
1 **pint blueberries**
2 **peaches, apples or pears,
   peeled and diced**
2 **teaspoons grated lemon
   peel**

1. In a saucepan, combine the spices, honey, lemon juice and simmer for 5 minutes.
2. Stir in the blueberries, peaches and lemon peel. Heat to boiling.
3. Reduce heat and simmer 5 minutes. Serve hot or cold.

Makes about 3 cups of relish

Smoked Fish Fillets

The gentle, moist heat of smoke-cooking is absolutely perfect for fish. The delicate flavor of fish welcomes the subtle addition of smoke; the texture of smoked fish is firm but very tender. Smoke-cook fish that you have caught, or use fish from the frozen food case. You can flavor the brine with any of the ingredients given below, or not use any additional flavoring at all — the choice is yours.

About 4 pounds fresh or thawed frozen fish fillets (you can smoke-cook less than this if you like)

1 quart cold water

⅓ cup plain salt or 3 tablespoons plain salt and 2 tablespoons seasoned salt

1 tablespoon cider, white wine or tarragon vinegar

Any one of the following: ½ teaspoon dried dill weed; ½ teaspoon crushed basil or oregano; ½ teaspoon crushed anise or fennel seed; ½ teaspoon crushed tarragon; ½ teaspoon dry mustard, ½ teaspoon *fines herbes* or generous dash hot pepper sauce

½ cup oil

About 4 Hours Before Serving

1. Arrange the fish fillets in a baking dish or heavy-duty plastic bag.
2. Combine water, salt, vinegar and any one of the seasonings suggested in a medium-size mixing bowl. Stir until the salt dissolves to make a brine.
3. Pour the brine mixture over the fish.
4. Cover with plastic wrap or close the bag securely.
5. Refrigerate at least ½ hour or up to several hours.
6. Start soaking 2 or 3 chunks of wood or a handful of wood chips, unless the smoker takes dry wood.
7. Fill the fire pan almost full with charcoal briquettes and start the fire.
8. When coals turn grey, drain the wood pieces and add them to the coals. (For electric units: unless the smoker takes dry wood, drain wood pieces and put them in their special pan.)
9. Set the water pan in place and fill half full with hot water.
10. Put the cooking grill in place.
11. Lift the fish fillets from the brine and rinse under cold running water. Add the brine to the water pan.
12. Brush the fish on both sides with oil, then arrange on the cooking grill.
13. Cover. (Plug in electric smoker.) Smoke-cook about 2 to 3 hours or until fish is firm to the touch or flakes easily when tested with a fork.

Makes about 8 to 10 servings

Apricot Cooler to go with Smoked Fish Fillets

Bring out the champagne glasses to serve this elegant treat. Apricot Cooler is a fitting finalé for Smoked Fish Fillets, a big tossed salad with avocados and sourdough bread.

1 can (15 ounces) apricot halves, drained

1 cup vanilla ice cream

6 tablespoons brandy

6 tablespoons creme de cacao

1 cup milk

6 ice cubes

6 sprigs fresh mint

1. Combine all the ingredients, except the ice cubes and mint, in a blender.
2. Blend until smooth.
3. Pour into chilled glasses.
4. Add an ice cube to each glass and garnish with a mint sprig.

Makes 6 servings

Smoked King Crab Legs

As an appetizer or for a main dish, King Crab Legs are superb. Add lemon juice, garlic salt or powder, or basil to the melted butter, if you want more flavor.

3 pounds thawed frozen Alaska King crab legs, split
½ cup butter, melted

About 1½ Hours Before Serving

1. Start soaking 2 or 3 chunks of wood or a handful of wood chips, unless the smoker takes dry wood.
2. Fill the fire pan about ³/₄ full with charcoal briquettes and start the fire.
3. When the coals turn grey, drain the wood pieces and add them to the coals. (For electric units: unless the smoker takes dry wood, drain the wood pieces and add them to their special pan.)
4. Put the water pan in place and fill about ²/₃ full with hot water.
5. Brush the crab meat with melted butter.
6. Set the cooking grill in place.
7. Arrange the crab legs, cut side up, on the cooking grill.
8. Cover. (Plug in electric smoker.) Smoke-cook about 1 hour or until the crab meat is white and firm.

Makes about 6 main dish or 12 appetizer servings

Brussels Salad to go with Smoked King Crab Legs

The key to this salad lies in steaming the Brussels sprouts just until they are tender, but still crisp. The tangy marinade and the vegetables complement Smoked King Crab Legs.

Salad
1½ pounds Brussels sprouts, steamed
2 medium onions, sliced
1 cup diced celery
¼ cup chopped pimiento

Dressing
¼ cup lemon juice
½ cup tarragon vinegar
¾ cup salad oil
1 teaspoon salt
1 teaspoon basil
½ teaspoon dry mustard
½ teaspoon pepper
¼ cup chopped parsley
½ cup chopped walnuts

1. Combine the vegetables in a bowl while the Brussels sprouts are still hot.
2. Mix together all the ingredients for the dressing and pour over the vegetables.
3. Cover and refrigerate for several hours or overnight.

Serves 8 to 10

Smoke-Cooked Shrimp

Absolutely, positively delicious! If you like garlic, add a minced garlic clove to the butter in the pan. If lemon is your choice, sprinkle in a tablespoon of juice, or slice a lemon to add to the pan.

1 pound peeled, deveined shrimp, thawed
¼ cup butter
½ teaspoon seasoned salt

About 1½ Hours Before Serving

1. Start soaking 2 or 3 chunks of wood or a handful of wood chips, unless the smoker takes dry wood.
2. Fill the fire pan about ¾ full with charcoal briquettes and start the fire.
3. When the coals turn grey, drain the wood pieces and add them to the coals. (For electric units: unless the smoker takes dry wood, drain the wood pieces and add them to their special pan.)
4. Set the water pan in place and fill about ⅔ full with hot water.
5. Put the shrimp and butter in a shallow metal pan or tray made from several layers of heavy-duty foil (be sure to turn up the sides of the foil to make an edge). Sprinkle with the seasoned salt.
6. Put the cooking grill in place and center the pan on the cooking grill.
7. Cover. (Plug in electric smoker.) Smoke-cook about 1 hour or until the shrimp is pink and firm.

Makes about 4 main dish or 8 appetizer servings

Fruit Baskets to go with Smoke-Cooked Shrimp

Here is a fancy way to present Smoke-Cooked Shrimp. The snappy grapefruit salad dressing contrasts delightfully with the shrimp.

Dressing

2 teaspoons cornstarch
½ cup water
¾ cup grapefruit juice
3 tablespoons oil
¾ teaspoon salt
1 teaspoon sugar
½ teaspoon paprika
½ teaspoon dry mustard

Fruit Baskets

3 large grapefruits
1 pound cold smoked shrimp
2 green onions, sliced thin
Crisp salad greens

1. Blend the cornstarch with the water in a small saucepan.
2. Cook and stir over medium heat until thickened.
3. Remove from the heat and stir in the grapefruit juice, oil, salt, sugar, paprika and dry mustard.
4. Beat until smooth. Refrigerate while making the fruit baskets.
5. Trace a line around the center of each grapefruit. To make zig-zag edges, insert a paring knife in the line at an angle to make one side of a point; cut through to the center. Pull out the knife and insert it at an angle to make the opposite side of the point. Continue cutting around the grapefruit. Pull the halves apart.
6. Cut around each section in each half, loosening the fruit from the membrane.
7. Remove the sections and mix with the shrimp and onion slices.
8. Cut out the core and membrane.
9. Line the grapefruit baskets with salad greens.
10. Mound the grapefruit sections, onion slices and shrimp in the baskets and drizzle with dressing to serve.

Makes 6 servings

SIDE DISHES

Two kinds of side dishes can be made in a smoke-cooker. One type goes right on the grill or in the water pan and takes on the same flavor as the main dish. The other kind is wrapped in foil and is not smoke-flavored. Either way, you will astonish your guests by producing a tasty dish from the smoker along with the main course.

Silver Turban Apples

Dessert can cook in the smoke cooker, along with your main course. Count on one apple for each guest, but cook a few extra, if you have room, to enjoy from the refrigerator a day or two later.

4 to 6 large baking apples
1 cup raisins or currants
⅓ cup honey
⅓ cup chopped nuts
¼ cup butter
   Pumpkin pie spice

About 2 Hours Before Serving
1. Wash and core the apples. If you wish, cut a strip of peel from the circumference of the apple so the skin will not split.
2. Tear off a 10-inch sheet of foil for each apple. Put an apple in the center of each piece of foil.
3. Fill the centers of the apples with the raisins, honey, nuts and a dab of butter. Sprinkle each apple generously with pumpkin pie spice.
4. Wrap each apple in foil, pressing and twisting the top to seal and form "turban."
5. Place the apples on the cooking grill along with the main dish for the last 1½ to 2 hours of smoke-cooking.

Makes 4 to 6 servings

Wash and core the apples. Tear off a 10-inch square of foil for each apple. Fill each apple with raisins, honey, nuts and a dab of butter. Sprinkle with spice.

Wrap each apple in a square of foil, pressing and twisting the top to seal the foil and make a silver turban.

Place the apples on the grill for 1½ to 2 hours of smoke-cooking.

Each Silver Turban Apple makes one tasty dessert. Serve the apples warm, with ice cream or whipped cream, if you like.

Curried Fruit

A fantastic side dish, curried fruit can cook on the smoke-cooker with beef or fish. If you do not have a casserole that will fit on the cooking grill along with other food, make one out of several layers of heavy-duty aluminum foil.

1 can (1 pound 3 ounces) cling peach halves or slices
1 can (1 pound 13 ounces) pear halves
1 can (1 pound 4 ounces) pineapple chunks
1 can (11 ounces) mandarin orange segments
½ cup maraschino cherries
¼ cup butter
½ cup brown sugar
1 tablespoon curry powder

About 1 Hour Before Serving
1. Drain the fruits, reserving the syrup for other uses, if you want.
2. Combine the fruits in a casserole or foil pan.
3. Dot with butter, then sprinkle with the brown sugar and curry powder.
4. Cover or seal the foil tightly.
5. Place the fruit on the cooking grill beside the main dish for last hour of cooking.

Makes 6 to 8 servings

Canned peaches, pears, pineapple, cherries and mandarin oranges have to drain before preparing Curried Fruit.

Combine the drained fruits in a casserole or pan and dot with butter.

Sprinkle the fruit with brown sugar and curry powder.

Cover the pan or seal it tightly with foil.

Place the fruit on the grill and smoke-cook for an hour. Curried fruit is delicious with beef or fish.

Asparagus in Foil

You can prepare other fresh vegetables this very same way. If vegetables are large, cut them into evenly-sized pieces for even cooking.

1 tablespoon butter
1 pound fresh asparagus, cleaned and trimmed
2 tablespoons water
2 tablespoons lemon juice
2 tablespoons Parmesan cheese, grated (optional)

About 2¼ Hours Before Serving

1. Tear off a 2-foot sheet of heavy-duty foil.
2. Spread the butter over the center of the foil.
3. Arrange the asparagus in the center of the foil.
4. Sprinkle with the water and lemon juice, then sprinkle with Parmesan cheese, if you want.
5. Bring the edges of the foil up and fold or pinch to seal securely.
6. Place the foil package on cooking grill beside the main dish for last 1½ to 2 hours of cooking.

Makes 4 servings

The ingredients for Asparagus in Foil are simple: butter, asparagus, water, lemon juice and Parmesan cheese.

Clean the asparagus and trim the tough ends before placing them on a 2-foot sheet of heavy-duty foil.

Arrange the asparagus in the center of the foil. Sprinkle with water and lemon juice.

Sprinkling a little Parmesan cheese on the asparagus adds an interesting flavor.

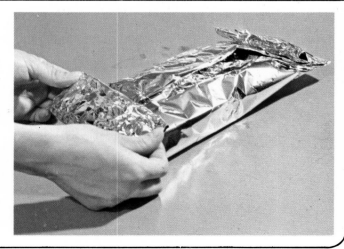

Bring the edges of the foil up and fold or pinch to seal securely.

Place the asparagus on the grill and smoke-cook for 1½ to 2 hours.

Garnished with additional lemon slices, Asparagus in Foil is a superb side dish.

Smoker Roasted Corn on the Cob

If you prefer your corn without smoke flavoring, husk and butter the ears, then just wrap them in foil before putting them on the grill. Plan on 1 ear of corn per serving.

Fresh, young corn on the cob (in husks, 1 per serving)
Butter, melted
Salt and pepper or an herb (dill weed or seed, tarragon, fennel or anise)

About 1³/₄ Hours, Before Serving
1. Carefully pull the husks back from the corn and remove the silk.
2. Brush the corn lightly with melted butter. Sprinkle with whatever seasonings you like.
3. Put the husks back in place. If necessary, tie the husks at the top of the ear with a metal twist, rubber band or piece of string to hold husks in place.
4. Arrange the corn on the cooking grill around the outside edges.
5. Add the corn to the smoker for the last hour to hour and a half of cooking time.

1 ear equals 1 serving

Smoked Onions

These onions are so delicious you will want to cook them along with any main dish you have scheduled for the smoker. One softball-sized onion will make about 3 servings.

2 large, sweet onions, peeled
¼ cup butter
¼ cup melted butter
½ teaspoon salt
⅛ teaspoon pepper

About 3 Hours Before Serving
1. Slice the onions crosswise ¹/₂ inch thick.
2. Generously butter a shallow pan or a tray made from heavy-duty foil.
3. Arrange the onion slices in the pan and brush with melted butter.
4. Sprinkle with salt and pepper.
5. Add to cooking grill along with meat for last 2 or 3 hours of cooking time.
Note: You can sprinkle seasoned salt, celery salt or herb blends on the onions.

Makes 6 servings

Herbed Smoked Tomatoes

Delicately seasoned and flavored with smoke, tomatoes make a savory accompaniment to a smoked main dish. Count on 1 medium-sized tomato for 2 servings.

Firm but ripe tomatoes
Basil
Salt and pepper
Butter

About 1¹/₄ Hours Before Serving
1. Halve the tomatoes and generously sprinkle the cut surfaces with basil, salt and pepper.
2. Generously butter a shallow metal pan or a tray made from several layers of foil.
3. Arrange the tomatoes in the pan, cut side down.
4. Place the pan on the cooking grill along with the main dish for the last hour of cooking time.

1 medium-sized tomato equals 2 servings

Smoked Acorn Squash

If you prefer to cook your squash in the smoker, but not have it flavored with smoke, just be sure the cut portion of the squash is tightly covered with aluminum foil. You can also cook chunks of squash in the water pan. Cooking squash in the water pan is especially nice when smoking pork or sausage because the water pan catches smoke-flavored drippings. One medium-sized squash will make 2 servings.

Medium-sized acorn squash (1 per 2 servings)
Butter, melted
Salt and pepper

About 2¼ Hours Before Serving
1. Cut the acorn squash in half and scoop out the seeds.
2. Brush the cut surfaces generously with melted butter, then sprinkle them with salt and pepper.
3. Arrange the squash on the cooking grill, cut side down.
4. Cover and smoke-cook about 2 hours or until tender.

1 medium-sized squash equals 2 servings

Smoker Mushrooms

If a shallow metal pan will not fit on the cooking grill, form heavy-duty foil into a tray to fit on the cooking grill next to the main dish. Plan on about 4 delicious servings from 1 pound of mushrooms.

1 pound large fresh mushrooms
¼ cup butter

About 1¼ Hours Before Serving
1. Wipe off the mushrooms or wash and drain them.
2. Cut off only the tip of the stem.
3. Lightly butter a foil tray or shallow metal pan, then arrange mushrooms in the pan.
4. Place the pan on the cooking grill along with the main dish for the last hour of cooking time.

Makes 4 servings

Creamy Grilled Potatoes

This potato dish probably will be so popular you will have to cook it along with every smoker-full of meat! You can vary the recipe by using another flavor of dry soup mix such as tomato or spring vegetable.

1 tablespoon butter
1 package (9 ounces) frozen French fries
1 cup dairy sour cream or sour half and half
1 packet dry onion soup mix

About 2¼ Hours Before Serving
1. Tear off a 2-foot sheet of heavy-duty foil.
2. Spread the butter over the center of foil.
3. Place the French fries in the center of the foil.
4. Top with the sour cream and then sprinkle with the onion soup mix.
5. Bring the edges of foil up and fold or pinch to seal securely.
6. Place foil package on the cooking grill beside the main dish for the last 2 hours of cooking.

Makes about 4 servings

Water Pan Potatoes

During the last hour of smoking, potatoes can cook in the water pan while the main dish smoke-cooks. The water pan should be only 2/3 full of water when you add the potatoes. Add them quickly so you don't cool off the smoker and set the cooking time back too much.

2 dozen tiny new potatoes

About 1 Hour Before Serving
1. Scrub the potatoes but do not peel them.
2. Slip into 2/3 full water pan under the cooking grill.
3. Cook along with the main dish for last hour of smoking time.

Note: In place of whole new potatoes you can use 4 to 6 large potatoes, peeled or unpeeled, quartered.

Makes 6 to 8 servings

Water Pan Potatoes, piled in a pyramid, are flavored with drippings from the main dish.

Silver Plated Carrots

You can cook any other root vegetable this same way — turnips, rutabaga, parsnips, for example. Do be sure to slice them or cut in thin strips lengthwise for even cooking.

1 tablespoon butter
1 pound carrots, peeled and sliced or cut into thin lengthwise strips
1 teaspoon sugar
½ teaspoon salt
½ teaspoon ground ginger or thyme
2 tablespoons water

About 2¼ Hours Before Serving
1. Tear off a 2-foot sheet of heavy-duty foil.
2. Spread the butter in the center of the foil.
3. Arrange the carrots in the center of the foil.
4. Sprinkle with the sugar, salt and ginger. Sprinkle with the water.
5. Bring the edges of the foil up and fold or pinch to seal securely.
6. Put the foil package on the cooking grill beside the main dish for the last 1½ to 2 hours of cooking.

Makes 4 to 6 servings

Garden on the Grill

For a delicious side dish, combine the best of the harvest in a foil packet to cook along with ribs, chicken, steak or any other main dish you are smoke-cooking.

4 tablespoons butter, divided
1 medium zucchini, sliced
1 medium yellow squash, sliced
2 medium tomatoes, chopped
1 medium onion, chopped
½ teaspoon salt
½ teaspoon basil
⅛ teaspoon lemon pepper

About 2½ Hours Before Serving
1. Tear off a 2-foot sheet of heavy-duty foil.
2. Spread 2 tablespoons of the butter over the center of the foil.
3. Place the two squash, tomatoes and onion in the center of the foil.
4. Sprinkle with salt, basil and pepper. Dot with the remaining 2 tablespoons of butter.
5. Bring edges of foil up and fold or pinch to seal securely.
6. Place the foil package on the cooking grill beside the main dish for last 2 hours of cooking.

Makes 6 to 8 servings

Elegant Green Beans

Serve this fancied-up vegetable with fish, turkey or beef.

1 tablespoon butter
1 package (10 ounces) frozen French-style green beans
1 can (4 ounces) sliced mushrooms or mushroom stems and pieces, undrained
1 teaspoon instant minced onion
½ teaspoon salt
Dash pepper

About 2¼ Hours Before Serving
1. Tear off a 2-foot sheet of heavy-duty foil.
2. Spread the butter over the center of the foil.
3. Arrange the green beans in the center of the foil.
4. Add the mushrooms, onion and seasonings.
5. Bring edges of the foil up and fold or pinch to seal securely.
6. Place the foil package on the cooking grill beside the main dish for last 1½ to 2 hours of cooking.

Makes 4 servings

Cook-Along Vegetable Casserole

This hearty casserole is a great accompaniment for beef, pork, or turkey. Drippings from the main dish flavor the casserole when you cook it on the second rack of a larger cooker or add a second grill to your smoker.

3 small zucchini, sliced
3 small yellow squash, sliced
2 cans (1 pound each) tomatoes, drained and chopped
1 package (20 ounces) frozen small whole onions
1½ teaspoons salt
1 teaspoon basil, oregano, dill or tarragon
2 tablespoons butter (optional)

About 4 to 6 Hours Before Serving

1. In a 3-quart casserole, combine both kinds of squash, the tomatoes and onions.
2. Sprinkle the vegetables with salt and the herb of your choice and stir to mix.
3. Dot with butter, if you wish.
4. Put the casserole on the lowest cooking grill, with meat above it, so the drippings can season vegetables.
5. Cover and smoke-cook along with the main dish during the last 4 to 6 hours.

Makes 6 to 8 servings

Smoker Beans

The old-fashioned beans cooked slowly in savory sauce are the greatest. You will need a bean pot or heavy, covered casserole for this recipe. You also need a stacking or doubling accessory to create a second cooking grill.

1 pound dried beans (Navy or Great Northern)
¼ pound salt pork or bacon, cubed
½ cup chili sauce
¼ cup molasses
1 medium onion, chopped
1 teaspoon dry mustard
1½ teaspoons salt

About 24 Hours Before Serving

1. Rinse the beans and pick out any bad ones. Put the beans in a pot or other large container and add enough water to cover.
2. Let them soak overnight or at least 8 hours.
3. Rinse the beans again and drain.
4. Put the beans and all the remaining ingredients in a bean pot or large covered casserole.
5. Add enough water to barely cover the beans.
6. Cover the pot or casserole and put them on the lower cooking grill.
7. Cover the smoker and smoke-cook 12 hours, or until the beans are tender.

Makes about 6 to 8 servings

Easy Smoked Beans

Pork and beans turn into a fancy side dish when heated in the smoker along with the main course.

1 can (1 pound) pork and beans
1 tablespoon chili sauce
1 tablespoon molasses
1 tablespoon minced onion
½ teaspoon dry mustard

About 2¼ Hours Before Serving

1. Combine all the ingredients in a small metal pan, casserole or bowl made from several layers of heavy-duty foil. Do not cover.
2. Put the pan on the cooking grill along with the main dish for the last 2 hours of cooking time.

Makes 4 servings

Fruited Rice

A versatile side dish, you could use apple or pineapple juice in place of the orange juice.

1 **cup regular rice, uncooked**
1 **teaspoon grated orange or lemon peel**
2 **cups orange juice**
½ **cup raisins**
½ **cup chopped nuts or thin-sliced celery**
1 **tablespoon instant minced onion**
1 **teaspoon salt**

About 4 Hours Before Serving
1. Tear off 2 feet of heavy-duty foil.
2. Mold the foil in the bottom of a medium mixing bowl, then lift it out to make a foil bowl.
3. Put all the ingredients in the foil bowl, then bring the edges together and pinch to seal.
4. Carefully place the foil package on the cooking grill seam-side up, beside meat, chicken or fish.
5. Smoke-cook about 3 to 4 hours.

Makes about 6 servings

Rummy Pineapple

A fantastic dessert to serve after a smoked pork roast, ribs, ham or turkey. You can substitute ½ to 1 teaspoon of rum extract for the rum, if you wish.

1 **ripe fresh pineapple**
3 **tablespoons rum**
2 **tablespoons butter**
2 **tablespoons lemon juice**
2 **tablespoons brown sugar**
¼ **teaspoon cinnamon**

About 1 Hour Before Serving
1. Cut the top from the pineapple and discard.
2. Cut the pineapple into quarters, lengthwise. Remove the core.
3. Cut the pineapple from the skin in one piece, then cut the fruit into bite-sized pieces. Replace the pieces on each quarter.
4. In a small saucepan, heat the remaining ingredients until the butter melts. Stir to blend.
5. Tear off 4 pieces of foil just large enough to wrap around each quarter of pineapple.
6. Place each quarter in center of a sheet of foil. Brush generously with the butter-rum mixture.
7. Bring the edges of the foil up and fold or pinch to seal.
8. Place the foil packages on the cooking grill beside the main dish for the last 45 minutes of cooking.

Makes 4 servings

Brandied Bananas

After you have amazed your guests with a smoked main dish, pull off another coup by serving a dessert from the smoker.

6 **bananas**
3 **tablespoons apricot jam**
3 **tablespoons brandy**
3 **tablespoons butter**

About 1 Hour Before Serving
1. Tear off an 18-inch sheet of heavy-duty foil.
2. Peel the bananas and cut them in half lengthwise.
3. Arrange the bananas in center of foil.
4. Spoon the jam over the bananas, then sprinkle them with the brandy and dot with the butter.
5. Bring the edges of foil up and fold or pinch to seal securely.
6. Put the foil package on the cooking grill beside the main dish for the last 45 minutes of cooking.

Makes 6 servings

SMOKE-FLAVOR

The flavor of hickory or other wood can be added to some foods without actually cooking them. Smoke-flavored nuts are the best known, but you can smoke-flavor seeds, eggs and cheese for delightful appetizers. Smoke-flavoring works best in a charcoal smoker with low-burning coals.

You can smoke-flavor cheese, nuts, salt, even eggs. By smoke-flavoring food, those who own charcoal smokers get extra mileage out of the charcoal because smoke-flavoring uses the low coals left after cooking the main dish. Savory smoke-flavored foods make tasty gifts, snacks or appetizers for other meals.

Charcoal Smokers

Smoke-flavoring food in a charcoal smoker requires low coals and the removal of the water pan. You can start your preparations for smoke-flavoring about an hour before the main dish is done, so the food to be smoke-flavored can go on the grill right after you take out the main dish.

1. About 1 hour before the main dish is done, or whenever the coals are low, start soaking a handful of chips or several chunks of wood in enough water to cover them. For a stronger smoke flavor use slightly more wood.

2. Prepare the food for smoke-flavoring as the recipe directs.

3. When the main dish is done, lift out the food and serve.

4. Remove cooking grill and set aside.

5. Lift out the water pan. Use the juices for gravy or discard. Set the water pan aside to clean later on.

6. Lift the soaked wood from water and shake well to drain. Arrange the wood on the coals.

7. Put the cooking grill back in place.

8. Arrange the prepared food on the cooking grill, leaving space between each piece of food. If you are smoke-flavoring small pieces of food that might slip between grill wires, arrange food on several layers of foil. Poke small holes in foil with a two-tined fork so the smoke can get through.

9. Cover and smoke-flavor several hours or for the time given in the recipe.

10. When the flavoring time is up, remove the food from the cooking grill. If the fire pan is cold, discard ashes, reserving any charcoal that may remain. If the fire pan is still warm, let coals die out or smother them before discarding.

Electric Smokers

In an electric smoker you can smoke-flavor foods at any time, not just at the end of the cooking period. However, smoke-flavoring usually takes less time in the electric units, because the heat level is the same as for smoke-cooking. Remember to leave the water pan in place when smoke flavoring in electric models.

1. Soak a handful of chips or several chunks of wood in enough water to cover them, unless the manufacturer directs you to use dry wood for smoking. For greater smoke flavor, use slightly more wood.

2. Meanwhile, prepare the food for smoke-flavoring as the recipe directs.

3. Lift the soaked wood from the water and shake it well to drain. Arrange the wood in special pan. (Or add dry wood to special pan.)

4. Put water pan in place and fill it half-way with hot water.

5. Put the cooking grill in place and arrange the food on the cooking grill, leaving space between each piece of food. If you are smoke-flavoring small pieces of food that might slip between grill wires, arrange the food on several layers of foil. Then poke small holes in foil with a two-tined fork so the smoke can get through.

6. Cover and plug in the smoker. Smoke-flavor for about 1 hour or for the time given in recipe. Because temperatures will be higher in an electric smoker than in a charcoal smoker with dying coals, check foods that might melt (such as cheese) after about half an hour.

7. When flavoring time is up, unplug smoker and remove the food from the cooking grill.

Smoked Nuts

What is your favorite nut? Cashews, almonds, pecans, walnuts? Whatever your choice, you can easily smoke-flavor nuts and the results are impossible to stop nibbling.

About 1 cup shelled nuts
¼ **cup oil or melted butter (optional)**
½ **teaspoon salt (optional)**

After Smoke-Cooking Other Foods

1. Start soaking 2 or 3 chunks of wood or a handful of wood chips, unless your smoker takes dry wood.
2. Make a shallow tray of several layers of foil, then poke tiny holes evenly across the bottom of the tray so the smoke can reach the nuts.
3. Drain the wood pieces and add them to the coals remaining in the fire pan. (For electric units: put the wood pieces in their special pan.)
4. For charcoal smokers: put the cooking grill in place but do not insert the water pan. For electric smokers; fill the water pan with hot water, insert it, then set the grill in place.
5. Put the tray on the cooking grill and pour in the nuts, arranging them in an even, single layer over the tray.
6. If you wish, brush nuts with oil and sprinkle with salt.
7. Cover. (Plug in electric smoker.) Smoke-flavor for 3 to 4 hours. In a charcoal smoker, you can leave the nuts in overnight or until the coals are completely dead.

Makes 1 cup serving

Smoked Salt

By smoking your own salt you can add smoke flavor to food anytime you like. Doing your own is very easy and, of course, much less expensive. Try it on popcorn!

Plain table salt

After Smoke-Cooking Other Foods

1. Start soaking 2 or 3 chunks of wood or a handful of wood chips, unless your smoker takes dry wood.
2. Make a shallow tray of several layers of foil.
3. Pour salt into the tray or the pan until just thick enough to cover the surface of the pan evenly.
4. Drain the wood pieces and add them to the coals remaining in the fire pan. (Electric smoker: place the wood in its special pan.)
5. Put the cooking grill in place but do not insert the water pan. (Electric smoker: fill the water pan with hot water and insert it; then set the cooking grill in place.)
6. Put the tray of salt on the cooking grill.
7. In a charcoal smoker, cover and smoke-flavor for several hours or until the salt is nicely tanned. You can even leave the tray in a charcoal smoker overnight or until coals are completely dead. (Electric smoker: plug in, cover and smoke-flavor the salt for up to 1 hour. Check the salt at intervals to make sure it is not getting too brown.)
8. Pour the salt into a container and cover tightly.
9. Use smoked salt to season meats, dips, salads or almost anything you like.

After smoke-cooking other foods, remove the water pan. The water pan is not used to smoke-flavor foods in charcoal smokers.

Add soaked wood chunks or chips to the low-burning coals.

Prepare a foil tray with holes in the bottom for the nuts. Spread the nuts in a single layer. Brush with oil or butter, if you wish.

Prepare a foil tray (no holes) for salt. Pour the salt into the tray in a layer thick enough to cover the tray's surface evenly.

Smoke-flavor the salt for up to 1 hour. The nuts may take 3 to 4 hours.

Smoked Cheese

After you smoke-flavor cheese, you can wrap the blocks of cheese in foil and refrigerate them to have on hand for parties or for special gifts. Cut pieces of cheese no thicker than an inch, so the smoke flavor can penetrate. Smoke-flavoring cheese requires very low heat and is not recommended in an electric smoker. However, directions for smoke-flavoring cheese in an electric smoker are given in case you want to experiment. Watch the cheese carefully so it does not melt.

Mild-flavored cheese, such as Colby, Monterey Jack, Muenster or cream cheese.

After Smoke-Cooking Other Foods

1. Start soaking 2 or 3 chunks of wood or a handful of wood chips, unless your smoker takes dry wood.
2. Make a shallow tray of several layers of foil or use a shallow metal pan. Poke holes in the foil.
3. If cheese is not in slab shape, cut it into large chunks no thicker than 1 inch and arrange the chunks on a tray or in a pan.
4. Add the wood to the coals remaining in the fire pan. The coals should be fairly low, because if the fire is still very hot, cheese will melt completely. The cheese will melt around the edges, but you do not want it to become completely liquid or to boil and toughen. (Electric smokers: place the wood in its special pan.)
5. Set the cooking grill in place but do not insert the water pan. (Electric Smoker: fill the water pan with hot water and insert it; then set the cooking grill in place.)
6. Place the tray of cheese on the cooking grill.
7. In a charcoal smoker, cover and smoke-flavor the cheese for several hours or until cheese is richly browned and flavored. (Electric smoker: plug in, cover and smoke-flavor the cheese for up to 1 hour. Check at intervals to make sure the cheese is not melting.)
8. Serve the cheese while it is still warm or let it cool slightly and then wrap it tightly in plastic wrap or foil and chill.
9. Let the chilled cheese stand at room temperature about an hour before serving.

After smoke-cooking other foods, remove the water pan. Poke holes in a foil tray.

Cut the cheese to be smoke-flavored into chunks no thicker than 1 inch.

You can smoke flavor different kinds of cheeses at the same time.

Smoke-flavor the cheese for several hours, until the cheese is richly browned.

Smoked cheeses make tempting appetizers to serve before a smoked dinner — or anytime.

Smoke-Flavored Seeds

Those people who love to nibble on sunflower, squash or pumpkin seeds will adore smoke-flavored seeds. You can buy hulled sunflower seeds at the supermarket or health food store. Save the seeds from your Jack O'Lantern; rinse and then dry them in a low oven before smoke-flavoring them.

About 1 cup sunflower, squash or pumpkin seeds
¼ cup oil or melted butter (optional)
½ teaspoon salt (optional)

After Smoke-Cooking Other Foods

1. Start soaking 2 or 3 chunks of wood or a handful of wood chips, unless your smoker takes dry wood.
2. Make a shallow tray out of several layers of foil, then poke tiny holes evenly across the bottom so the smoke can reach the seeds.
3. Drain the wood pieces and add them to the coals remaining in the fire pan. (For electric units: put the wood pieces in their special pan.)
4. For charcoal smokers: set the cooking grill in place but do not insert the water pan. For electric smokers, fill the water pan with hot water and insert it, then set the grill in place.
5. Set the tray on the cooking grill and pour in seeds; arrange them in a single layer.
6. Drizzle the seeds very lightly with oil or melted butter and sprinkle with salt, if desired.
7. Cover. (Plug in electric smoker.) Smoke-flavor the seeds for 3 to 4 hours or until the light-colored seeds turn medium-brown. Give the seeds a taste test: if you can taste the smoke flavor, they are done.
8. Cool the seeds and store them tightly covered.

Makes 1 cup

Joe's Jerky (Charcoal Smokers Only)

Keep jerky on hand for quick snacks at home, or to pack in bike bags, backpacks, knapsacks or lunch bags. You might want to experiment with other marinades for the meat and pick the one your gang likes best. People who like to snack on jerky at home usually prefer the soy or teriyaki sauce, but that version may be a little too salty for backpackers on hikes with limited water supplies.

1½ pounds flank steak or top round steak

½ to ¾ cup soy or teriyaki sauce, steak sauce or Worcestershire sauce

The Night Before Serving

1. Put the steak in the freezer until it is almost frozen.
2. Remove the steak from the freezer and cut it in very thin strips across the grain. Cut away and discard any fat or connective tissue.
3. Place the steak strips in a heavy-duty plastic bag.
4. Pour the sauce over it and toss the strips to coat each piece.
5. Close the bag securely or cover the dish tightly and refrigerate several hours or overnight.

After Smoke-Cooking Other Foods

1. Remove the water pan and set it aside; it will not be used.
2. Put the cooking grill in place.
3. Lift the meat from the marinade and arrange it in a single layer on the cooking grill.
4. Cover and let the meat dry over low coals about 6 to 8 hours, overnight or until meat is dried. The jerky should be just a little flexible and very chewy.

NOTE: You can add soaked wood to the low coals before putting the meat on the cooking grill, if you want smoke-flavored jerky.

Makes about 6 to 8 appetizer or snack servings

Smoked Eggs

Smoked eggs? Yes! You can smoke-flavor hard-cooked eggs to make an unusual snack or appetizer. Remember that you should hard-cook, not hard-boil the eggs. Cover them with water; bring the water to a boil; cover and remove the pan from the heat and let it stand for about 17 minutes. Cool the eggs under cold, running water, then refrigerate or peel them.

Chilled, peeled hard-cooked eggs

After Smoke-Cooking Other Foods

1. Soak 2 or 3 chunks of wood or a handful of wood chips, unless the smoker takes dry wood.
2. Drain the wood pieces and add them to the coals remaining in the fire pan. (For electric units: unless the smoker takes dry wood, drain the wood pieces and place them in their special pan.)
3. For charcoal smokers: put the cooking grill in place but do not insert the water pan. For electric smokers: fill the water pan with hot water, insert it, and set the grill in place.
4. Arrange the eggs on the cooking grill.
5. Cover. (Plug in electric smoker.) Smoke-flavor the eggs about 20 to 30 minutes or until they are lightly browned.
6. Remove the eggs from the grill. Cut them in half to eat immediately, or wrap whole eggs in plastic wrap or foil and refrigerate them to enjoy later.

½ egg equals 1 appetizer serving

OTHER COOKING METHODS

Slow-cooking is just one of the other cooking methods possible with a smoke-cooker. You can use either a charcoal or electric smoker to roast just like a conventional oven set on high. If you have a charcoal smoker, you can use it as a broiler. Slow-cooking, or steaming, can be done in both types of smoke-cookers. It is the same process as smoke-cooking, only you do not add wood. Roasting eliminates both the wood and the water pan, as does broiling.

Slow-Cooking (Steaming)

By eliminating the wood chips usually added to the fire pan, you can slow-cook foods without adding smoke flavoring. Some of the smoker manufacturers refer to this as "steaming," although we feel that word is not quite accurate. (We prefer slow-cooking.) Slow-cooking is nice when you are tired of smoke-flavored foods, or when you would like to cook delicately flavored foods, such as fish, shrimp or lobster. The following recipe can be used as a model for other slow-cooked foods. Check the instructions that come with your cooker in case there are any special directions.

Slow-Cooking Lobster Tails and Corn on the Cob

Corn on the cob (1 per serving)
Butter
Lobster Tails (1 per serving)

1. For a charcoal smoker, put the fire pan in place, fill with charcoal and light the coals.
2. Put the water pan in place and fill completely.
3. While waiting for the coals to turn grey (about 20 minutes), remove the silk from the ears of corn. Brush the corn with butter. Replace the husks, tying the tips in place, if necessary.
4. Put the first grill in place above the water pan and arrange the lobster tails on it.
5. Put the second grill in place and arrange the corn on it.
6. Cover. (Plug in electric smoker.) Cook for 1 to 2 hours or until the lobster flesh is white and firm. Note that the only difference between slow-cooking (steaming) and smoke-cooking is the absence of wood chips.

For slow-cooking, or steaming, you eliminate the wood chunks. Fill the water pan with water.

Place the lobster tails (or whatever you want to cook) on the grill in a single layer.

Add a second grill for cooking more food.

AND OTHER COOKING METHODS

Arrange the corn (or other food) on the second grill. Cover and cook for 1 to 2 hours. In general, cooking times are twice as long as in a conventional oven.

Lobster Tails and Corn on the Cob are delicious when slow-cooked.

138

Broiling (Charcoal Smokers Only)

You can broil in a charcoal smoke cooker by using less charcoal in the fire pan and moving the fire pan up to the water pan position. Eliminate the water pan and set the cooking grill directly over the fire pan. We suggest only a single layer of two coals in the fire pan for broiling, otherwise the heat is just too intense. Also we found there is considerable flaming as fat from meat falls onto the coals. So, while it is possible to broil in the smoker, we think broiling is better done on an appliance designed especially for that purpose. The following recipe is a model for other foods to be broiled. Check the instructions that come with your cooker. We do not recommend broiling with an electric element in a smoke cooker. The heat is too high and there is too much flaming.

Broiling Strip Steaks

Strip Steaks

1. Arrange a single layer of coals in the fire pan.
2. Put the fire pan in the water pan's position.
3. Ignite the coals and let them burn until covered with grey ash.
4. Put the grill in place directly above the fire pan.
5. Arrange the steaks (or fish or other broilable items) on the grill and broil, turning once, until they are as done as you like.

To use a charcoal smoker as a broiler, use a single layer of coals in the fire pan.

Place the fire pan in the water pan's position closer to the grill. Light the coals.

When the coals are covered with grey ash, put the grill in place.

Arrange the steaks (or other broilable food) on the grill in a single layer. Broil, turning once, until the food is done to your taste.

Broiled Strip Steaks, a tossed salad, rolls and watermelon. What more could you want!

Roasting

You can do a nice roasting job in both electric and charcoal smoke-cookers. To roast, just leave out the water pan and do not add wood chips. The fire pan goes in its regular position and the cooking grill in its regular position. Roasting temperatures in the smoke-cooker are high (about 450°F to 500°F, or even higher at the beginning of the cooking period), so this type of roasting is good only for large, tender pieces of meat, such as thick steaks or whole beef tenderloins. The recipe for Peppered Rib Roast is the model for roasting other foods. Also, check the instructions that come with your smoker.

Peppered Rib Roast

Pepper
Standing Rib Roast (¼ to ½ pound per serving)

1. For a charcoal smoker, put the fire pan in place, fill with charcoal and light the coals.
2. Pepper the roast on all sides.
3. Insert a meat thermometer in the roast.
4. Put the grill in place and set the rib roast in the center of it.
5. Cover. (Plug in electric smoker.) Cook for the length of time given in standard recipes for roasting at high temperatures (450°F to 500°F). For a rib roast, cook it 10 minutes per pound. Cook to rare or medium-rare only. Note that you do not use the water pan at all.

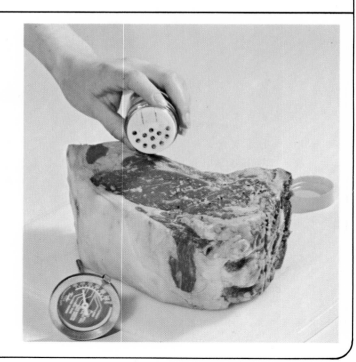

For roasting, eliminate the water pan and wood chunks. Prepare the food to be roasted. Rib roast is simply sprinkled with pepper.

Insert a meat thermometer away from any bone.

Place the food on the grill once the charcoal is ready.

Peppered Rib Roast makes a stunning main course.

GRAVIES, MARINADES AND SAUCES

Savory drippings from the main dish collect in the water pan. Wonderful gravies can be made from those drippings, so don't discard them. The gravy will be doubly delicious if you have added any excess marinade to the water pan before smoke-cooking. If there is not enough liquid in the water pan, you can augment it with bouillon cubes and still enjoy smoke-flavored gravy.

Great Gravy from the Water Pan

The juices that drip from the food on the grill into the water pan are delicious. To capture their goodness, you can reserve the juices in the water pan and thicken them for sauce or gravy.

Juices from the water pan
1 tablespoon fat from water pan or butter for each cup gravy
1 tablespoon flour for each cup gravy

1. Carefully lift the water pan out of the cooker and carry it to the kitchen. Wear protective mitts or use thick pot holders.
2. Pour the juices into a 1-quart glass measure or deep, heat-proof bowl.
3. Skim or pour off fat, reserving 1 tablespoon for each cup of gravy you will be making.
4. Measure the liquid, reserving 1 cup for each cup of gravy you will be making. If you have less than 1 cup of liquid, add water to make a cup. If you added water to the pan during cooking time and juices seem diluted, pour the liquid into a saucepan and boil briefly to reduce it. You can also add a bouillon cube or two, or a teaspoon or two of instant bouillon to juices that do not have quite enough flavor.
5. For each cup of gravy, heat 1 tablespoon skimmed fat (or butter) in a saucepan.
6. Add 1 tablespoon flour for each cup of gravy and blend. Cook and stir until the mixture is frothy.
7. Add the reserved liquid from the water pan.
8. Cook and stir over medium-high heat until the mixture comes to a boil and is smooth and has thickened.
9. Serve the gravy with the meat.

Makes at least 1 cup of gravy

Wearing oven mitts, carefully lift the water pan from the smoker and carry it to the kitchen.

Pour the juices into a 1-quart glass measuring cup.

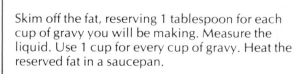

Skim off the fat, reserving 1 tablespoon for each cup of gravy you will be making. Measure the liquid. Use 1 cup for every cup of gravy. Heat the reserved fat in a saucepan.

Add 1 tablespoon flour for each cup gravy. Cook and stir until frothy. Add the measured liquid from the water pan. Cook and stir until the gravy boils and is smooth and thick.

Cornstarch-Thickened Gravy

If you prefer to save some calories, skip the fat and thicken the water pan juices with cornstarch.

Juices from the water pan
1 tablespoon cornstarch for each cup gravy
1 tablespoon cold water for each cup gravy

1. Skim the fat from the water pan juices and reserve 1 cup of the liquid for each cup gravy, just as in directions for Great Gravy from the Water Pan.
2. For each cup gravy, in small bowl combine 1 tablespoon cornstarch with 1 tablespoon cold water and blend until smooth.
3. Add the reserved liquid and cook and stir over medium-high heat until the mixture comes to a boil and is smooth and has thickened.
4. Boil and stir 1 minute.

Makes at least 1 cup of gravy

AU JUS
Skim the fat from the juices in water pan. Spoon the juices over the meat.

For each cup of gravy, combine 1 tablespoon cornstarch and 1 tablespoon cold water.

Add the measured liquid from the water pan.

Cook and stir until the gravy boils and is smooth and thick.

MARINADES AND SAUCES

Basic Barbecue Marinade

For rich tomato flavor and deep brown color it is hard to beat this easy combination of savory and sweet ingredients. It also makes a great basting sauce for meats or fish. The recipe makes enough for 2 pounds of kabobs, 3 to 4 pounds of ribs, 4 to 6 lamb shanks or a 5 pound beef roast.

⅔ cup catsup or chili sauce
⅓ cup red wine or cider vinegar
3 tablespoons molasses or brown sugar
2 tablespoons instant minced onion
1 teaspoon Worcestershire sauce
¼ cup water
1 teaspoon salt
1 teaspoon dry mustard
Dash hot pepper sauce

Combine all the ingredients in a medium bowl.

Makes about 1½ cups

Lovely Lemon Marinade

Fish, chicken, ribs and ham have a delicate, slightly oriental flavor after soaking in this marinade.

1 tablespoon grated lemon peel
½ cup lemon juice
⅓ cup soy sauce
¼ cup oil
1 bay leaf, crushed
½ teaspoon lemon pepper

Combine all the ingredients in a medium bowl.

Makes about 1½ cups

Savory Soy Marinade

Pork chops, pork steaks, fish steaks, turkey legs or ducklings take on an oriental flavor when marinated in this spicy concoction.

½ cup soy sauce
⅓ cup oil
⅓ cup sherry, sake, or red or white wine vinegar
¼ cup finely chopped green onion
1 clove garlic, minced
½ teaspoon ground ginger
½ teaspoon dry mustard

Combine all the ingredients in a medium bowl.

Makes about 1½ cups

Tomato Marinade

Tomato marinade gives chicken, turkey, fish or ribs or a beef steak a rich brown color and delicious flavor.

1 can (8 ounces) tomato
    sauce
¼ cup lemon juice
2 tablespoons water
2 teaspoons sugar
2 teaspoons Worcestershire
    sauce
1 clove garlic, minced
1½ teaspoons salt

Combine all the ingredients in a medium bowl.

Makes about 1½ cups

Easy Sweet-Sour Marinade

This marinade adds a zippy flavor to fish steaks, turkey, chicken or pork. The recipe makes enough for 4 pounds of country-style or regular spareribs.

1 cup orange marmalade
½ cup soy sauce
¼ cup sherry or cider
    vinegar
1 clove garlic, minced
2 tablespoons oil

Combine all the ingredients in a medium bowl.

Makes about 2 cups

Cold Hot Sauce

Even though you chill this easy sauce, it is plenty hot to the tongue. Serve it with smoked chicken, turkey, pork, beef or fish. It is especially tasty with plain smoked meats that have not been marinated.

4 medium tomatoes,
    peeled, chopped and
    drained
1 can (4 ounces) green
    chilies, seeded and
    chopped
1 tablespoon instant
    minced onion
1 tablespoon chopped
    fresh parsley or cilantro
    or ½ teaspoon ground
    coriander
½ teaspoon garlic salt
½ teaspoon salt

Combine all ingredients in a medium bowl and chill thoroughly.
Note: Whip an 8-ounce package of cream cheese, then stir in ½ cup Cold Hot Sauce for a superb dip.

Makes about 2 cups

MARINADES AND SAUCES

Easy Onion Marinade

Beef roasts, pork chops, lamb chops, chicken or turkey pieces are complemented by onion flavoring. For the most flavor, pour the marinade over meat and refrigerate overnight. If you are in a hurry marinate meat at room temperature for just an hour. The recipe makes enough marinade for a 5-pound roast or 2 chickens.

1 **envelope onion soup mix**
1 **cup oil**
2/3 **cup vinegar (use tarragon, white or red wine, or cider vinegar)**
2 **tablespoons finely chopped parsley**
1/4 **cup soy sauce**

Combine all the ingredients.

Makes about 2 cups

Terrific Tarragon Marinade

Tarragon is great with turkey, chicken or fish. Be sure to crumble the leaves between your fingers to get extra flavor. Makes enough marinade for 2 chickens or 3 or 4 pounds of fish.

3/4 **cup oil**
2/3 **cup tarragon or white vinegar**
1 **to 2 tablespoons dried tarragon, crumbled**
1 **teaspoon salt**
1/2 **teaspoon garlic powder**

Combine all the ingredients.

Makes about 1 1/3 cups

California Cheese Combo

Put a generous dollop of this peppy mixture on top of smoke-cooked burgers, steaks, fish, even smoked roast beef. It also makes a great filling for omelets, for grilled sandwiches or over hot, cooked vegetables. Try it, too, as an appetizer, with smoked cheese or nuts and an assortment of crackers.

1 1/2 **cups shredded Cheddar cheese**
1 1/2 **cups shredded Swiss cheese**
2/3 **cup dairy sour cream or mayonnaise**
1 **can (4 1/2 ounces) chopped pitted ripe olives**
1 **jar (4 ounces) pimientos, drained and chopped**
2 **tablespoons finely chopped green chili peppers**

Combine all ingredients in a medium mixing bowl. Cover and store the cheese in the refrigerator. Let it stand at room temperature 20 to 30 minutes before servings.

Makes about 1 quart

Almost Instant Cherry Sauce

Serve this easy-to-make sauce with ham, pork or turkey for an elegant meal. The recipe makes enough to serve with a 6 to 10 pound ham or turkey.

1 can (21 ounces) cherry
    pie filling
1 teaspoon grated lemon
    peel
¼ cup lemon juice
½ teaspoon cinnamon or
    allspice

Combine all the ingredients in a medium saucepan and heat to boiling. Keep hot to serve with the meat.

Makes about 2 cups

Cumberland Sauce

A great sauce for smoked turkey, duck, ham or tongue, Cumberland Sauce has a sweet-sour tang. It will keep in the refrigerator for several smoke-cooked feasts.

⅓ cup red currant jelly
⅓ cup orange or lemon
    juice
⅓ cup Port wine

Combine all ingredients in a medium saucepan and heat until the jelly melts.

Makes about 1 cup

Mint Sauce

Mint is an obvious choice for smoked leg of lamb, but this sauce is also surprisingly good with turkey or fish. Substitute grape jelly and try it with hot dogs — kids love it!

⅔ cup mint jelly
⅓ cup lemon juice
1 tablespoon chopped
    fresh mint or parsley
¼ teaspoon salt

Combine all the ingredients in a medium saucepan and heat until the jelly melts.

Makes about 1 cup

Sweet and Hot Sauce

You can increase or decrease the "fire" in this sauce by using more or less hot pepper sauce.

¾ cup apple jelly
1 tablespoon instant
    minced onion
1 tablespoon minced green
    pepper
3 tablespoons lemon juice
    or white vinegar
¼ teaspoon hot pepper
    sauce

Combine all the ingredients in a medium saucepan and heat until the jelly melts.

Makes about 1 cup

Smoker Products Mr. Meat Smoker Models 171 and 371

TEST REPORTS

Charcoal or Electric

Which is best for you, charcoal or electric smoker? It depends on how you live. If you are going to do all your cooking in the back yard or on the patio, never venturing away from an electric outlet, then an electric model may be ideal.

If you spend vacation time camping, or if you want a smoke cooker that can go away with you, then a charcoal model is the better choice. We suggest one of the smaller models, if you intend to travel with it.

Several manufacturers offer smokers with slip-out electric elements that can be used to convert charcoal models to electric models — a handy option.

The even, consistent heat and the convenience of the plug-in operation are the main advantages of electric units. Manufacturers suggest electric units can be used indoors. We think an open garage is indoors enough, because the cooking odors are strong. Savory though it may be, you may not enjoy your home smelling like smoked turkey for several days after the cooking. There is some condensation and dripping, so any surface you use the electric smoke cooker on should be protected with a drip pan, several layers of newspaper or a piece of foil.

If you live where days with temperatures over 70°F happen only a few months of the year, an electric unit will let you enjoy smoked foods throughout most of the colder months. It is nice to smoke-cook a turkey for the winter holidays and have the range oven free for other goodies.

Electric units usually give food a subtler smoke flavor that charcoal models, since the wood chars slower. So, if a strong smoke flavor is important to you, a charcoal model might be your best choice.

Charcoal smoke-cooked foods seem to come out of the cooker a little browner, as well as more richly smoke flavored than those cooked in electric units. Smoke-flavoring, as distinct from smoke-cooking, works better over the lingering, low coals of a charcoal unit. The constant, higher heat of electric units may melt cheese, for example.

The disadvantages of the charcoal cookers are the variables of cooking times and the slight mess that comes with handling charcoal, lighter fluid, ashes, etc. However, you can use charcoal models for broiling; broiling in electric smokers causes excessive flaming and is not recommended.

Size is an important consideration when it comes to charcoal models. Those with big families, or who frequently have big picnics or patio parties, may opt for the stack attachments that provide another cooking grill, or for those models that have 2 cooking grills built in. These units are handy for cooking two kinds of meat, as well as vegetables.

The size of the charcoal pan itself determines how much and how long you can cook. As a rule of thumb, most charcoal smoke cookers will cook for about 1 hour per pound of charcoal (with a minimum of five pounds of charcoal in the pan). This means that a small model, such as the Mr. Meat Smoker's Mandarin unit, cannot handle an eight-pound turkey, whereas the big Cajun Cooker can take on a sizeable chunk of meat. Buy the size you will need.

The cost of cooking is another consideration. Ten pounds of charcoal, at this writing, cost around $3.00. Ten hours of electricity to operate a 1250 to 1500 watt electric element now costs 50 to 60 cents at four cents per killowatt hour. Of course, prices of both these fuel sources vary widely throughout the country and can change considerably. If cost is an important factor in which type you choose, check charcoal and electric prices for your locality.

Accessories

What options should you add to your smoke cooker? Some of that decision depends, of course, on what is available for the model you buy. The decision also depends on how you cook and how much you want to spend.

Stack Attachment. If you entertain frequently, or have a large family, then seriously consider the larger cookers or a stack or doubling attachment. The stack or doubling accessory provides an extra cooking grill, with an accompanying ring to expand the height of the cooker itself.

Rib Rack. If ribs are a favorite of yours, then also consider buying a rib rack. This useful rack holds the ribs on end and allows you to place many more servings on the grill than if the slabs of ribs were laid flat. Some rib racks also have skewers along the sides, to hold potatoes for cooking.

One model, the Cook'n Ca'jun, had a grill-like extender to create another level of cooking.

Work Table. A work table that slips over the top of some Smoke'N Pit models looks helpful, but it tends to unbalance the unit, so you must be careful not to overload one side or the other of the work table.

Electric Element. An electric heating element to convert a charcoal smoker to electric is a convenient option, we think, giving you a choice of heat sources.

Ash Guard. An ash guard or drip pan will help protect your patio or terrace. Although a piece of foil or newspaper will do the job just as well, the ash guard is more permanent and more attractive.

Test Reports

Smoke cookers are specialized appliances. The job they do best is smoke-cooking, even though charcoal models can be used for broiling and both charcoal and electric units can be used for roasting. This means that the ease of smoke-cooking, and the flavor of smoke-cooked foods, must be something you especially like because smoke cookers are considerably more expensive than simple charcoal braziers.

In addition to the dollar investment in a smoke cooker, you have to invest space — space on your patio or terrace to use the smoker, and space to store it when it is not in use. You will also need space for charcoal storage, too, unless you select an electric model.

Once you have accepted those investments, you are ready to select a smoker cooker. The brand and model you choose may depend on what is available in your area. Most brands have national distribution, but that does not mean that your local hardware store will handle any of them. It may take some searching.

All the brands and models we tested were acceptable. All of them smoke-cooked foods in about the same amount of time. Some models could handle larger amounts of charcoal, and, therefore, larger amounts of food.

It is up to you to determine your smoke-cooking needs. If your family is small, if you do not plan on big parties or gatherings that feature smoke-cooked foods, and if you would like a handy and portable smoker, then consider the Mandarin Meat Smoker by Smoker Products.

But, if you plan to entertain a lot, if you want to

cook a turkey, some ribs and some vegetables all at once, then look for a double grill model, such as the Cook'n Ca'jun (the biggest of them all), or the Kelley, Smoke 'N Pit or Country Cooker models with double grill or stacker accessories.

Smoker Products Mr. Meat Model 171

This attractive smoker is the single grill model of Smoker Products line. The double grill model is 271; the electric model 371 has UL approval.

Similar in appearance to the Smoke 'N Pit, the Mr. Meat 171 has a large fire pan that holds 12 pounds of charcoal. The water pan holds three quarts and it has cooking grills 15 inches in diameter. A hole in the base of the fire pan provides air for the fire. The rim of the top is notched to hold four skewers.

Recently improved, the grill and water pan are held in place by a wire bracket for easy access to the charcoal pan and for cleaning up. The wire bracket lifts out by handles that extend over the top rim. The Mr. Meat Smoker cooked well in all tests. We did find the temperature gauge in the cover of the Mr. Meat 171, and 471, less than accurate. In all our testing the gauge never got above the range labelled "Warm" and into the "Cook-

ing" range, even though food was cooking well and finished in the usual period of time.

Smoker Products Mr. Meat Model 471

This deluxe, two-grill model performed as well as the 171. The model 471 does have an added feature that we found convenient; a door in the side of the unit lets you check the water pan and add charcoal to the fire pan (although only one briquette at a time) without having to raise the cover. The 471 also has its grill and water pan held in place by the removable wire bracket and the notches for skewers. A set of four skewers comes with all double-grill Mr. Meat Smokers.

Smoker Products Accessories

The Mr. Meat Electric Adapter EA is a handy accessory, allowing you to convert any charcoal unit to electricity. The adapter was easy to slip in and out of both Mr. Meat units tested. There is enough "ease" around the edges of the electric unit that condensed steam can run down the sides of the smoker and not collect, as in the Smoke 'N Pit electric. It maintained the proper, even cooking temperature. Other accessories available from Mr. Meat include skewers, a drip pan, rib rack, electri-

Smoker Products Mr. Meat Smoker Model 271

Smoker Products Mr. Meat Models 471 and 571

cal extension cord, hickory blocks, and preferred wood (oak and pecan) and Mr. Meat Smoker Seasoning. A stack and cooking grill to convert the single grill smoker into a double unit is also available. Each unit comes with a slim, well-prepared information and recipe booklet.

Smoker Products Mandarin Meat Smoker

The baby of the smokers we tested, the Mandarin is a compact little unit that is small enough to be portable. The Mandarin's charcoal pan holds six pounds of briquettes, enough to cook chicken, ribs or a small roast (less than five pounds). The water pan holds three quarts and the cooking grill is 13½ inches in diameter. The low unit is black, lightweight, easy to cook in and easy to move around, but it will not maintain cooking temperatures for more than four or five hours, so you are limited as to the kind of foods and amounts of food you can cook.

We found that, after considerable testing, the paint around the rim of the Mandarin began to peel, undoubtedly from condensation of steam that collects at the junction of the cover and the body of the unit.

It did perform well in our tests but, because of its small size, and because of the paint peeling, the Mandarin comes in last in our selection of recommended cookers.

Smoke 'N Pit 2200 Series

Smoke 'N Pit 2200 is an electric smoker, available in a small one-grill model or taller two-grill model. The single-grill model consumes 550 watts; the double-grill uses 1250 watts. Both have eight-foot, three-pronged cords. These units plug into a standard 110-Volt outlet and do a superb job of maintaining a low, constant, cooking temperature. The water pan holds 1 gallon of liquid. Our tests showed that there is no need to add water to the water pan every four hours, an important point for fuss-free smoke-cooking.

The 14-inch diameter cooking grills have fold down handles, a particularly convenient feature, we think. We did find some problems with liquid condensation while working with the electric Smoke 'N Pit. Although the manufacturer does supply a small bag of ground clay to sprinkle over the bottom of the unit, there tends to be more moisture than the clay can absorb. We think the bottom of the smoker should be wiped out or drained after each use, to keep it dry. We did not do this in our initial tests and found that the moisture remaining in the bottom encouraged mold and rust. Another problem with condensed

steam is caused by the cover which is designed so that drips run down the outside rather than the inside of the main cylinder making unsightly stains on the attractive exterior.

Smoke 'N Pit has designed a handy work table that fits across the top of the electric unit. We particularly appreciate the convenience of a "landing" area for food and tools. The double grill model Smoke 'N Pit is tall, however, and can be tipped, especially with the table in place. Smoke 'N Pit's promotional materials say it can be used inside or out. We suggest a garage or breezeway is as close to indoors as you want to get, unless you are going to omit the addition of wood. Although subtle and pleasant at the beginning, the aroma of the wood will linger when you smoke inside. If you do smoke-cook inside a garage, be sure to put the unit on its ash guard or several layers of newspaper to absorb the condensation that drips down the outside of the unit.

With these few minor exceptions we found the electric Smoke 'N Pit one of the best of the electric models. Both charcoal and electric Smoke 'N Pits come with an excellent instruction and recipe booklet.

Smoke 'N Pit 2200 Series

Smoke 'N Pit 2100 Series

This is the charcoal model of Smoke'N Pit. It has a good-sized fire pan that holds 12 pounds of briquettes and a water pan that can hold one gallon of liquid. The 15½-inch cooking grill can hold a meal-sized load. You can cook a 12-pound turkey successfully in the Smoke 'N Pit.

An attractive unit, the Smoke 'N Pit comes in black, orange, brown or yellow. You have to do some assembling, attaching the legs and putting the handsome wood handles in place. A screwdriver and a pair of pliers are all it takes.

The Smoke 'N Pit has a low profile, which means it is not likely to tip over, but also means you do have to stoop to work with it. You do need to check the water pan after four hours of cooking and add more water, if necessary.

A Smoke 'N Stack unit with a cooking grill is an optional and handy accessory to convert the Smoke 'N Pit to a double-grill model. You can buy the stack in colors to match the Smoke 'N Pit. Other accessories, all of them useful, are an ash guard, a rib rack, and six and 25 pound bags of hickory or mesquite chunks. Three-pound bags of hickory chips are also available.

The Smoke 'N Pit cover is designed to fit inside the base, allowing condensation to drip down the inside of the smoker. That is an important point in appearance; drips that run down the outside of the smoker are difficult to clean off. The Smoke 'N Pit units, and all the accessories, are made of heavy-duty metal, are sturdy and performed very well in all our tests.

Smoke 'N Pit units are made by the Brinkmann Company, who also produce a very similar, but less expensive line of charcoal and electric smokers called Country Cookers.

Cook'n Ca'jun

Cook'n Ca'jun charcoal smokers come as a Double Grill Smoker, Model S80, or a single grill, Model S60. Of all the smokers we tested, these two models have the largest charcoal pans and water pans. The size of these pans is, we think, a great advantage. The charcoal pan holds 15 pounds of briquettes and the water pan 2½ gallons when full to the brim. The larger the charcoal pan, the longer you can cook. The large charcoal pan is particularly important if turkey or large cuts of meat are on your menu. The big water pan

Smoke 'N Pit 2100

Smoke 'N Pit Country Cookers

is important for the same reason: you do not have to interrupt the cooking by lifting the lid to check the water level and adding more water. (All other models, except the Smoke'N Pit electric, need water added after about four hours of cooking.)

The Cook'n Ca'jun has, in addition to the cooking grills and water and fire pans, three separate parts: a base to hold the fire pans, a main body and the cover. This construction lets you reach the fire pan without having to lift it in and out of the deep cylinder, as in some other models. The base that holds the fire pan is vented to assure even burning and also is designed so that ashes remain in the base and do not spill out on your patio or lawn.

A step-up grill is available to further increase the cooking area. This is an optional accessory. The Cook'n Ca'jun has a very handy heat indicator in the handle of the cover. During testing, the indicator gave accurate indications of the cooking temperatures inside.

The Cook'n Ca'jun comes in black, green or red, has large (15½-inch diameter) chrome cooking grills and heat resistant handles. The unit sits low to the ground and is quite stable.

If you are looking for a smoker to handle big loads of food, we recommend the Cook'n Ca'jun.

Kelley Big Boy Charcoal Water Smoker

The Kelley unit has long legs that bring it up to a comfortable working height. Although it comes unassembled, the Kelley unit has clear, specific directions and requires only a screwdriver, a pair of pliers and a few minutes of your time to assemble. The Kelley charcoal pan is big (although not as big as the Cook'n Ca'jun) and holds 12 pounds of charcoal. The water pan holds about 1 gallon.

The Kelley is designed with air holes in the bottom of the cooking chamber, so air can get in, but ashes cannot get out. A "Doubler" accessory converts the single-grill Kelley to a double-grill model. Because Kelley's cover is a nice high dome, there is plenty of room for a big bird or roast to fit underneath.

Kelley also makes an electric cooking element to convert the charcoal unit to electricity. The UL approved unit comes with clear instructions for installation and use. When using the electric adapter you do need to add water to the water pan, just as in the charcoal models, so plan to check the pan every 4 hours or so and add water as necessary. The Kelley electric element is well-designed and easy to put in place.

We recommend Kelley charcoal and electric smoke cookers. Both performed well in all our tests.

Cook'n Cajun Model S60

Kelley Big Boy Model 1600

INDEX